BETH NYHART

# REND YOUR HEART & NOT YOUR GARMENTS

To all the people who walked with me
out of slavery and into the light.

# Table of Contents

Foreword by Pastor James Reed

# Foreword

For over thirty years I have served the Body of
Christ as a local church pastor. I've done so in five
states, across three denominations, and in a couple
of community churches, as well. I have had the
immense privilege of walking beside hundreds of
men and women of all ages at all stages of
Christian development. And countless times these
precious friends came to a grinding halt on their
faith journeys because of something the
contemporary Western Church has not addressed
effectively: SIN. Some parts of the Church have
tended to address it from a legalistic perspective,
adding condemnation and striving to those already
burdened by the shame of the sin in their lives.
Other parts of the Church have preached a grace
message that downplays the devastating
consequences of ongoing sin in a life. All too often,
that grace message ignored the liberating truth of…

Titus 2:11-12 (NRSV)
*"For the <u>grace</u> of God has appeared, bringing salvation to all, <u>training us to renounce</u> impiety and worldly passions, and in the present age to live lives that are self-controlled, upright, and godly..."*

True grace never excuses sin. That is like a doctor excusing cancer. But true grace does something far better. It enables. It enables a Christ-follower to forsake sin, and to experience the joy and freedom that comes from living a life in which sin truly does not have dominion over us (Romans 6:1-11).

I've never met Beth Nyhart. I'm only writing this because of a connection that came about through a mutual friend. But I know Beth Nyhart. And by the time you finish this book, you'll know her, too. Her heart and soul are laid bare on every page. There's no pretense. In fact, there is at times an uncomfortable level of candor. But it is the candor of a prophet, of one who has heard God say something to her spirit, and now that word has become a fire in her bones. Make no mistake, it is a cleansing fire. But her message is not fiery. It's stark, but kind. Insightful and incisive, yet nonetheless inviting. Beth is like a doctor who refuses to sugarcoat a life-threatening diagnosis

8

because she knows only a full understanding of the nature of the disease will inspire the patient to do the hard work of healing. And her "treatment protocol" is right on target. Drawing from both her own life experiences, a rich repository of classic Christian texts, and the best kind of Biblical scholarship (that is, the kind done by one who needs an answer or they can't go another step)...Beth lays out a path to freedom and wholeness. If you have the courage, you'll come out on the other side of this book better able to recognize, turn from, and live above sin in your life than you were before you started. And if you're like me, you will agree that's a payoff worth pursuing.

James Reed
Lead Pastor, New Life Community Church
Danville, VA

*Introduction*

# There's a Porn Addict in Your Church

*"Do you not know that if you present yourselves to anyone as obedient slaves, you are slaves to the one whom you obey, either of sin, which leads to death, or of obedience, which leads to righteousness?"*
*Romans 6:16*

I don't feel qualified to write this book, but I recognize that as a tactic Satan uses to keep God's children subdued. So I'll ignore that sick feeling for now and plow ahead. First I want to share my story--my testimony of what God has done in my life--because that is the only qualification I really have in all of this. I am a born again Christian. I am a believer in Jesus Christ as the Son of God, the Holy Bible as the inspired word of God, and I'm also a porn addict.

Pornography was introduced to me at 8 years old in the form of a magazine left along the bank of the Conewago Creek in South Central Pennsylvania where I grew up. I was instantly hooked, the way some people become addicted to a substance as soon as they try it. This was not the first time I was curious about sex or the first time that I had tried masturbation, but it was the first time that I felt that ugly trance of fascination. I soon came to connect that feeling with lust, which for me in childhood was a mindless grasping for pleasure.

Around the same time I accepted Jesus into my heart... again. I was one of those kids who prayed the sinner's prayer 487 times just to make sure it stuck. But I remember the night I sat in my bed looking out at the streetlights below and recognized I needed to have faith that God would keep His promise to save me if I confessed and believed. I prayed once more that night and never looked back.

Growing up in the 90s, my older brother was interested in computers and we had access to the internet long before my parents really understood the danger of it. My fascination with sex had been limited to masturbation, fantasies, and romance novels, but that dial-up connection opened up a whole world of depraved people searching for others of a like mind. I frequented chat rooms that seemed innocent until someone sent you a private message.

As this was going on, I was also being raised in a Christian home with parents who loved me and taught me the scripture. I became very involved in my church and youth group, gained a position on the church board, led the youth drama team, live worship band, and was held up as an example to my peers.

I hope you can see this back-and-forth theme. I was living double lives. I would be determined to follow Christ and then turn around and succumb to lust. My body was a machine and I fed it every time it asked. My conscience was becoming seared. I cried out to God asking Him to heal me, but time and time again He answered by asking me to do the one thing I couldn't even comprehend.

*Confess.*

No. God and I were at a stand-still. He had come as far as I was willing to let Him, and now I was giving Him a hard pass. I would NOT go to my parents or youth leaders who thought I was amazing and completely ruin all the faith they had in me. Surely there was another way.

*Obey me.*

No. I knew in my heart that you can't correct your course by continuing in the wrong direction; you have to turn around and go back to where you went wrong in the beginning. I understood this. But in my mind I created scenarios where it was good enough that God and I knew the extent of my sin, and somehow, if I kept moving forward, everything would end up alright.

*Trust me.*

No.

My dad asked us to memorize Romans 6, which held a lot of meaning for him, and I remember speaking these words and hardening my heart against the Spirit's voice:

*What shall we say, then? Shall we go on sinning so that grace may increase? By no means! We are those who have died to sin; how can we live in it any longer? Or don't you know that all of us who were baptized into Christ Jesus were baptized into his death? We were therefore buried with him through baptism into death in order that, just as Christ was raised from the dead through the glory of the Father, we too may live a new life.*

*For if we have been united with him in a death like his, we will certainly also be united with him in a resurrection like his. For we know that our old self was crucified with him so that the body ruled by sin might be done away with, that we should no longer be slaves to sin— because anyone who has died has been set free from sin.*

I didn't understand what "set free from sin" meant. I couldn't imagine a life without pornography in it. I wanted to be free from the shame and compulsions, but sin had me in a grip so tight that I felt certain I would never live without its fingers around my neck. Enslaved to sin was my reality. I knew exactly what that meant. It meant that I obeyed my flesh, no matter what my spirit told me to do. It meant that I silenced my spirit and obeyed my slave master.

The phrase Rend Your Heart & Not Your Garments comes from Joel 2:13 where the prophet is pleading with Israel to return to the Lord. They couldn't skate by on an outward appearance of repentance or obedience anymore, God was demanding a broken and humble heart.

When I was seventeen I realized I was never going to break free. And maybe it was the teenage hormones, but I decided I needed to do something drastic. I had been considering a small discipleship program based at a retreat center in Spring Creek, Pennsylvania, and I decided to give myself an ultimatum. Either I would attend the Miracle Mountain Ranch Apprenticeship Program [1] and confess my past, or I was going to remove myself from all Christian leadership and openly pursue the things of the world that I couldn't let go of.

In the fall of 2005 my family dropped me off at the Ranch and drove the 250 miles back home. I had been researching all of the staff because I knew that students were assigned to a staff couple as their advisors for the year. These were going to be the people I confessed all of my dark secrets to, and I had a few favorites. But God had something different in mind. I was assigned to Chip and Sandy Hungerford, a quiet and unassuming couple who did not meet my imagined ideal of the strong spiritual leaders who would help me break the curse of sin in my life. I cringe now at my pride and thank God for their strength and commitment to me over the next years.

It took me two weeks to work up the courage. I met with Sandy in the basement of their house with her large family running around upstairs, and I let go of everything I had been hiding so carefully for the past decade.

Honestly, I had hoped that confession would be the magical switch that would heal me. But that just wasn't the case. I was in for another decade of hard work, setbacks, victories, terrible mistakes, and humbling my heart before God. He led me along the same narrow path which He brings all of His followers. The lessons He taught me weren't new or revolutionary; but over those next 10 years God laid in my heart the foundation for this book and prepared me to be a messenger to church leaders today.

In Biblical times a prophet went to the people and relayed a message from God. If you read through the Old Testament you will find hundreds of verses where God pleads with His people to come back to him. Now, I'm no prophet. But God has burdened my heart with a plea for my brothers and sisters in Christ to pay attention to what He has already revealed to us in His word.

The question is, are you willing to listen to Him?

For the longest time, I was not. But I have purposed never again to say no when He asks me to trust him. I pray that you make that same commitment as you read these pages.

*Come.*

Yes, Lord.

*Chapter One*
# Teaching Kids About Sin

*"Daughters of Jerusalem, I charge you: Do not arouse or awaken love until it so desires."*
*- Song of Solomon 8:4*

Teaching our kids to deal with sin is a lot like teaching them to go to the bathroom. It's a fact of life, and we all do it. Because if we let that waste build up inside, we would get sick and die. Our bodies require that cleansing to function. In the same way, our spirit requires a way to get rid of the ugly nasty gunk of sin that is a normal result of living in a fallen world. So, help your kids learn that keeping your conscience clear is just as necessary as keeping your bodies clean.

My parents were a consistent wise voice in the years I spent enslaved to sin. After a few months at the Ranch I was able to confess to them what had been going on in my life and they were shocked and upset thinking that they had failed me in some way. But in reality, my sinful behavior was in spite of everything they had exemplified to me so well. I relied on that steadfast and straightforward example of obedience and faithfulness in ways they probably still don't realize.

One of my mom's regular teachings was based on the verses in Song of Solomon, where the bride is urged not to awaken love too early; later on in the book she is told to be like a wall. My mom encouraged me to protect my heart like a walled garden, not like a door that was open to any young man who wanted to come in and look around.

When I was in my early 20s she wrote me this letter on the subject:

> *In the Song of Solomon, we are repeatedly warned not to "awaken my love before she pleases". I believe this is a reference to the passions....we are not to be sexually active in thought & heart until it is appropriate to be sexually active physically. This is why modesty is an issue...not just clothing, but thought & behavior. You can be incredibly immodest and completely covered up...it is easy to entice with glances & smiles. It is why we are told to guard our hearts....the books we read, the things we watch, the*

*friendships we cultivate. At the end of the book, Solomon talks of a little sister...and the need to be a wall rather than a door. If you want an intensely satisfying sexual life with your future husband, YOU MUST BE A WALLED GARDEN with only one way in–marriage.*

*The result of my being a "door" was like having a broken cistern in my heart. I had all kinds of hunger & thirst for attention & affection but no way to keep my bucket full. I was like that verse in Proverbs 27:7, "A sated man loathes honey, but to a famished man any bitter thing is sweet." In the margin below that verse I wrote this years ago–"If I am not content in His love, I'll be tempted to "be content" filling the gap with food, attention, fantasy–and if He has not already filled me, those comparatively bitter things are sweet. But if I'm content in Him I will not idolize."*

*No matter what you are in life, you will have "hunger pangs"–unfulfilled desires. It is easy to think that something you don't have will satisfy you, but what actually happens is more like a meal; it fills you up for a short time. If you're eating junk then you will be full for a short time but not get any benefit from it...it will cause harm. It really is like that verse in Proverbs: if you learn to be content with God, your life is full even when you have nothing. If you are starving for God, you eat & eat & eat all the world has to offer & keep getting hungry again because nothing the world has satisfies forever even though it tastes sweet at the time.*

Children are being exposed to the ugliest things in our world at younger and younger ages, many times in ways that parents have no idea are going on. We're living in a world obsessed with feeling good, and our kids are going to see that and emulate it as they interact with the world around them.

Our gut reaction can be to shelter kids from outside influences in an effort to preserve their innocence. Child and teen ministries can be full of warnings about worldly things to avoid, but they can provide very little practical advice to kids (or parents) about how to do that.

So, what is the answer? How can you steer children away from sin when they are bombarded by it from every angle? How do you combat the things kids see in school, the media, family members, internet time, TV, and protect them from all of the random and unpredictable temptations which you as a parent have zero control over?

You can't.

From what I have observed, none of the methods that parents use to separate their kids from worldly influence and temptation do that great of a job. We shouldn't be surprised by this, however, because each kid has his or her own sin nature and desperately wicked heart. In Mark 7 Jesus tells his disciples, *"What comes out of a person is what defiles them. For it is from within, out of a person's heart, that evil thoughts come..."* The outside influence may give them ideas, but sin doesn't need to be taught. Human beings are sinners from birth, and so we need to expect our kids to act like sinners.

The most effective way to teach a child to deal with sin in their heart is to show them how you deal with sin in yours.

✚

You can prepare your children for the realities of sin by being intentional about how it is handled in your home. You need to set the expectation that sin is a normal part of life, and you need to set a precedent of how it will be confronted.

You **set the expectation** that sin is a problem for every human on earth, and it is not surprising or alarming to you that they will sin. Set the expectation that you are the one they can come to with questions, and let them know those conversations will be confidential and non-judgmental. Have these conversations regularly, and in both formal and informal settings. In fact, set the expectation that you care about their thought life even more than you care about their grades.

When our daughters start approaching puberty we talk to them about how their bodies will change. We want them to be prepared so their period doesn't take them by surprise. Some parents will pack their daughters an emergency period kit just in case it happens while they are away from home.

How much more should we prepare our kids for the realities of dealing with their sin nature? This is something we know with 100% certainty will affect them, that there is literally an enemy at war for their minds and souls, why would we let them walk into that blind?

In Deuteronomy 6 and 11 Israel is instructed to teach the commandments to their children, talking about them and bringing them up in conversation constantly. This could be by asking them about their motives in a situation, it could be by discussing how an advertisement or song on the radio aligns with God's word, or it could be frankly speaking about when you are tempted to sin so they understand temptation is something normal and they can learn to combat it.

As a church leader you can set the expectation that your ministry encourages families to talk openly about sin and temptation, and offer classes training parents how to implement those discussions in their homes.

For example, my young daughter has developed a habit of asking me every time she does something wrong if I still love her when she is bad. At her age this is a great opening to a conversation about how my love for her is not based on her performance. We talk about how Jesus died for us while we were still sinners, that he loved us that much even when we do bad things.

Setting an expectation of openness around sin looks like...

- Making sure kids know that all humans sin
- Emphasizing that their sin does not change your (or God's) love for them
- NOT speaking condescendingly about others who sin
- Apologize, confess, and ask forgiveness when you sin against your kids
- Explain and exemplify the concepts of grace and repentance
- Regularly discuss how culture aligns or conflicts with scripture

The other side of this is **setting the precedent** for what dealing with sin looks like. A precedent is *"something done or said that may serve as an example… to justify a subsequent act of the same or an analogous kind."* [2] A precedent for how to deal with sin means that you show them by example the proper way to do it.

This is your job, and it's hard to showcase what you see as a weakness in yourself. But kids see what you do, and what you do matters far more to them than what you say. If you tell them that they need to deal with their anger but never show them what it looks like to deal with your own anger, you set a precedent of false righteousness.

Kids feel secure when you clearly define what you want from them. You set the precedent for all future interactions by your honesty, your transparency, and your obedience to God in this area. You are essentially saying, like Paul told the Corinthians, *"follow my example, as I follow the example of Christ"* (1 Corinthians 11:1).

Let that sink in.

Do not set yourself up as an example to a child if you are not willing to deal with your own sin.

Jesus says in Matthew 18:6 *"If anyone causes one of these little ones--those who believe in me--to stumble, it would be better for them to have a large millstone hung around their neck and to be drowned in the depths of the sea."*

Being a parent IS being a leader. And being a pastor or holding any other ministry role in a child or teenager's life is a weighty responsibility as well.

God has placed you in a position of greater responsibility because you have eternal souls in your care. James 3:1 talks about teachers being judged more strictly, and the context of that verse is interesting. The verses before it are about our actions (faith without deeds is dead), and the verses after are about our words (the tongue is a fire). When we tell children to follow our example, we had best make sure that we are first obedient ourselves.

Setting the precedent for how to deal with sin means going first to show them how it is done. When you obey God's prompting to go first, others will feel compelled and empowered to join in.

Setting the precedent means giving an example, so the child or teen knows how to follow. It means that you humble yourself first. Set the precedent for dealing with your sin by making it a routine part of Christianity.

Setting a precedent of dealing with sin looks like:

- Praying together for the Spirit to point out sin
- Confessing your sin (in age appropriate ways) to God and each other
- Discussing the (age appropriate) struggles of temptation
- Keeping one another accountable to change
- Taking their sin seriously
- Modeling what God's forgiveness looks like

When all is said and done, there is no way for us to know that any of our efforts are going to keep our kids from being entangled in sin. And really, it is better that way. The spiritual discipline of faith is one that I exercise daily as a parent, but I have never found such peace and joy than I do when I lay my child in God's hands.

Their eternal souls are precious to God. More precious than they are to us, which blows my mind. Satan will try to make you believe that you are in this battle for your kids alone. He might try to tell you that your own failures disqualify you from teaching them, or he might try to tell you that you need to hold on tighter and tighter until you have no trust in God's ability to guide your child at all. Both are lies. The God who created your child is developing a personal relationship with them and will draw them to Himself, using you, if you'll let Him.

Elisabeth Elliot puts it this way in her book *Passion & Purity*, *"Does it make sense to believe that the Shepherd would care less about getting His sheep where He wants them to go than they care about getting there?"* [3] Our kids are safer in His care than in our own.

So we have an enormous resource at our fingertips when it comes to helping our children avoid Satan's traps. We have the resource of prayer--a direct line to the all-powerful God who formed them in their mother's womb and cares about every hair on their head. This God has been leading His children out of sin and redirecting them to holiness from the moment they first disobeyed.

Our children and teenagers are our brothers and sisters in Christ. We are not responsible for their salvation, but we have been placed in a position of influence and we play a major role in God's work.

Ephesians 6 lists the full armor of God, and it has been pointed out that the only offensive weapon is the Word of God, followed immediately by a call to prayer. As parents, teachers, and leaders in these young one's lives, we are called to fight for them with scripture and with prayer. Lay your hands on them, study with them, speak the Word to them when you sit and lie down and walk along the way.

Prayer and scripture are powerful weapons against Satan and his demons, and you learn to wield them skillfully with daily practice. Pray for your children as if there is an enemy strategizing against their eternal souls. Pray for them habitually, urgently, and fervently.

# Reflect & Check

*Take a few minutes to pray about and answer these questions. Is God asking you to change, repent, or act differently as a leader or as a Christian?*

---

*How did you learn about the concepts of sin and confession? Did your family address them? How?*

*What is the precedent for dealing with sin in your home right now? Do you think it needs to change?*

*Do you know what sins your parents struggled with?*
*Do your kids know what sins you struggle with?*

# Chapter Two

# How God Defines Sin

*"How sick is your heart, declares the Lord God,
because you did all these things,
the deeds of a brazen prostitute."*
*- Ezekiel 16:30*

Any book about sin must be founded in the
abundance of scriptures that God saw fit to
dedicate to the subject. The Bible talks about sin *a
lot*. In the years I spent studying how sin works, I
have asked quite a few people what their definition
of sin was. So let me ask you...

Think of a definition for sin. Do you have one in
mind? Write it down:

Some definitions I have heard are: breaking God's law; anything that separates you from God, disappointing God. We tend to think of sin generically. We think of it as something that makes God sad or something that we don't want God to see, like a teenager hiding things from their parents. We water down our opinion of sin until it's this grayish, sort-of-bad-but-not-super-bad, vague thing that we know we should avoid but it isn't that big of a deal.

We have generalized sin to the point of minimizing it.

Patricia S. Klein wrote the introduction to *Virtue and Vice*; a collection of C. S. Lewis' writings from a variety of his books, and I love the way she addresses our tendency to strip words of their true power and meaning:

*"The word vice sounds benign, describing fundamentally harmless habits and attitudes, the kinds of things normal people do and feel. The word virtue, by contrast, communicates a prudish self-righteousness, the sort of character we're not interested in being around, much less becoming...*

35

*Both virtue and vice have been gutted, stripped of their power, and left empty of truth. Sadly, eviscerating the words does nothing to alter the conditions the words originally described, and then, more sadly still, we are left with no words to describe powerful and real matters. Without the words, how can we ever hope to learn, to understand, to change?"* [4]

When God talks about sin, He uses strong language. It's bad. It's personal. It's horrible and ugly. Throughout the Old Testament God uses sexual terms to speak about the broken covenant between Israel and Himself.

In Ezekiel 16, Jeremiah 2, and Hosea, God paints a graphic picture of a bride who leaves her husband and family over and over again to pursue sex with strangers. It is jarring to read. He uses the word "whore" to reference her 17 times in the Ezekiel passage. This is not a God who is merely disappointed by our sin. The chapter starts out with Israel as an abandoned newborn lying naked in a pool of birthing blood beside the road. He calls to her, "Live!" and he causes her to flourish and mature, and when she is at the age for love, he marries her.

Rather than being grateful to her rescuer and husband, the bride accepts all of his gifts and bears him children, then goes out looking for sex. She takes the gold, the fine clothes, and the rich foods that her husband, out of his love, gave her. She uses them to lure strangers to her bed. She even slaughters and sacrifices her children to satisfy her lust.

*"How sick is your heart, declares the Lord God, because you did all these things, the deeds of a brazen prostitute, building your vaulted chamber at the head of every street, and making your lofty place in every square. Yet you were not like a prostitute, because you scorned payment. Adulterous wife, who receives strangers instead of her husband! Men give gifts to all prostitutes, but you gave your gifts to all your lovers, bribing them to come to you from every side with your whorings."*
*Ezekiel 16:30-33 (ESV)*

I am always struck by this point-- a prostitute only performs sexual favors in exchange for payment, but the adulterous bride pays her lovers. She's not just cheating on her husband, she is offering men money and gifts to have sex with her. This is what God is saying our sin looks like. A wife who refuses to be content with her family but goes offering random men money to sleep with her, trying to fill her insatiable lust. This is what God compares Israel's betrayal of Him to.

How sick is your heart? How sick is mine?

The prophet Hosea was asked to become a living object lesson of this message to Israel. God says *"Go, marry a promiscuous woman and have children with her, for like an adulterous wife this land is guilty of unfaithfulness to the Lord."*

God uses sexual/adulterous terms because Israel understood the covenant of marriage and the significance of breaking that covenant. They needed to understand that their sin against God was breaking the covenant that He had made with them. Not just breaking it, but cheating on it over and over again, like the wife whoring herself out on a street corner.

Our covenant with God through Jesus' death and resurrection is different than the covenant He had with Israel in the Old Testament. But God still uses the visual of the marriage covenant to show us what that relationship should look like. We need pointed examples like this to understand the gravity of deliberately living in sin, which completely disregards and disdains the beautiful covenant relationship that we are in with our maker.

God uses strong language and graphic visuals when he describes sin. He is not just *disappointed*. He is *devastated*. Sin is a cancer. Sin is a homewrecker. Sin is rooting deep into His children's souls and keeping them from true fellowship with Him. God *hates* sin.

So why do we love it?

The Garden of Eden is where Earth and mankind were cursed, but that wasn't the first act of sin among God's creation. In Ezekiel 28, Isaiah 14, and Luke 10 you can piece together an account of the first occurrence of sin in the angel Lucifer's heart. Ezekiel 28:17 says *"your heart was proud because of your beauty; you corrupted your wisdom for the sake of your splendor."* What a chilling statement when compared to Ezekiel 16:15 (ESV) speaking about the adulterous bride, *"but you trusted in your beauty and played the whore.."*

Satan is not a creator. He may be the original sinner, but his abilities are limited to distorting the good things that God has made. In his heart he saw beauty as something that made him powerful, instead of recognizing it as a joyous gift from a loving creator. All too consistently we fall into the same trap.

If we can't take our sin as seriously as God does, we'll always struggle to understand His heart and His commands. We are so wrapped up in the pressure to feel good now, to feel vindicated now, to feel powerful now, that we push away from our Redeemer who saved us from so much. We turn to those things of the world that taste sweet in the moment, but ultimately we're ripping our lives apart instead of building them up.

In 1 John 2:16 (ESV), three different types of sin are outlined. *"For all that is in the world—the desires of the flesh and the desires of the eyes and pride of life—is not from the Father but is from the*

*world."* These three are major areas where Satan can get a foothold in our lives.

**Desires of the flesh** are most often linked to sexual sin but scriptural teaching about what our flesh desires adds much more to the list than just lust. Galatians 5 gives us these items: *"sexual immorality, impurity, sensuality, idolatry, sorcery, enmity, strife, jealousy, fits of anger, rivalries, dissensions, divisions, envy, drunkenness, orgies, and things like these."* I tend to use the term immorality to describe the desires of the flesh. Immorality is also generally used in the context of sexual sin, but the word by itself means the opposite of morality. It means to violate principles of right and wrong.

This is a sin I see in myself often. I am an over-indulger. If there is something good, comfortable, relaxing, delicious, thrilling, or fascinating I go beyond indulgence and just way over-do it. Immorality is the point at which the good things in life become more important to us than obedience, such as when the excitement of debate becomes a hunger to argue, when the satisfaction of taking a break becomes an unwillingness to get up and work again, when the pleasure of seeing physical beauty in a person becomes an ugly way to satisfy a sexual urge.

**Desires of the eyes** differs from desires of the flesh because it shifts away from the flesh's baser urges and focuses on the all-consuming need to acquire more. More money, more possessions, more prestige. This sin can be described as greed. Ecclesiastes puts it this way, *"Whoever loves money never has enough; whoever loves wealth is never satisfied with their income."* The rich young man in Matthew 19 is a lesson about the trap of hoarding resources for yourself instead of understanding that everything you have comes from and belongs to God.

I see greed in my heart when the money we make is not enough to keep me content. When I feel the push of desire to work more, make more, buy more. When I measure success by my accomplishments or possessions. I see it when I grumble about needing to budget but blow through money when it is available, and when I feel reluctant to tithe or give to someone in need.

**Pride of life** is a preoccupation with self. James and Peter both write *"God opposes the proud, but* *gives grace to the humble"* and there are verses about pride all throughout scripture. Pride has an attitude of "I deserve", and is consistently seeking to lift itself up. Lucifer's words right before his fall are *"I will ascend above the heights of the clouds; I will make myself like the Most High"* (Isaiah 14:14), and this is also the lie he told to Eve--that the forbidden fruit would make her like God.

Pride rears its ugly head every time I get up in arms about an injustice that has been done to me. Every time I forget that God controls my future and I push ahead with my own plan because *I deserve* to be appreciated, compensated, and understood. Every time I parade my success in hopes that others think highly of me. Every time I seek approval from man rather than from God.

These three categories of temptation show up again in Matthew 4 when Satan tempts Jesus in the wilderness. We know that Jesus was tempted in every way that we are tempted (Hebrews 4:15) so let's see how the temptations that Satan chose correspond to those that John warns about. He offers three different enticements:

1. "If you are the Son of God, tell these stones to become bread."
2. "If you are the Son of God, throw yourself down.."
3. "All this I will give you if you bow down and worship me."

When Satan tempts Jesus with his human desire of satisfying His hunger after a 40 day fast, he is asking Jesus to go against His moral principles and break His fast on Satan's terms. He is tempting Jesus to make an immoral choice--lust of the flesh.

When he dares Jesus to throw himself from the temple and quotes Psalm 91 saying the angels will save Him, he is asking Jesus to test God. He is tempting Jesus to react with an "I deserve ____ because of who I am" attitude--pride of life.

When Satan displays the kingdoms of the world and offers them to Jesus for the price of bowing down to worship him, he is asking Him to disobey God for the sake of material gain. He is tempting Jesus with a sin of greed--lust of the eyes.

God created man in His image and with His breath. He made man to be a caretaker for the rest of His creation. He blessed the man and woman and charged them to rule and subdue and populate the earth. Adam and Eve were in fellowship with God until they chose to listen to the talking snake and disobey His command.

We are a sinful people. We continually disregard the God who created us, provides for us, saves us, and invites us to be in fellowship with Him again. We are not satisfied with Him and we pursue the empty things of this world we think will make us happy. We take personal advantage of the forgiveness of sin without fully comprehending the depth and damage of sin.

We are the adulterous wife.

And until you can drop your pride and admit that, you will never really understand what sin is. You will never really understand what you have been saved from. You will never really understand the significance of what Christ did for you.

I am the whoring bride. So are you.

# Reflect & Check

*Take a few minutes to pray about and answer these questions. Is God asking you to change, repent, or act differently as a leader or as a Christian?*

———

*Has your definition of sin changed from reading this chapter? How would you define sin now?*

*Which sin type (lust of the flesh, lust of the eyes, pride of life) do you see in yourself the most?*

*Ask God what is a recurring sin for you*
*and write down what He says.*

*Chapter Three*
# What Sin Should Look Like

*"For the sinful nature desires what is contrary to the Spirit, and the Spirit what is contrary to the sinful nature. They are in conflict with each other, so that you do not do what you want."*
*- Galatians 5:17*

It has always surprised me how unprepared we are when we encounter sin in the church. From the 3rd chapter of the Book this has been a gigantic problem with all of humanity. Why would we not expect to encounter it? Why are we not better equipped to handle it?

Even if someone is not hiding a bondage to sin, there are certain general characteristics of being a Christian with a sin nature that are going to look the same. These characteristics are normal, par for the course, and should be regularly addressed in your church and teachings.

## The Spirit and the flesh will be at odds

I once read a book about a girl who had another being occupying her body. They were both conscious, able to hear each other's thoughts and, every once in awhile, the foreign being could wrestle control of the body and enact things against the girl's will.

As I was reading this I kept thinking... in a weird way, this is what having the Spirit and a sin nature is like. At times there is a literal war going on because your sin nature, the Holy Spirit, and you are all occupying the same body. The Spirit convicts and prompts you in directions that your sin nature is vehemently opposed to. And the thing is, you should be able to see that war in people. Seeing the Spirit and flesh in conflict is a good indication that this person is aware of and dealing in some way with their sin nature.

The conflict between Spirit and flesh can look like:
- A balance of selfish and selfless choices
- Apologies for offenses and true effort to correct them
- Frustration with the desire to choose sin

- Willingness to talk about struggles past and present (in the proper setting)

What you want to see in a person's life is the evidence of that sin nature. If you don't see any evidence of a sin nature, they are intentionally hiding it. This doesn't mean that you go asking every person in your congregation about their struggles, but provide opportunities for people to share, whether in small groups, classes, or one-on-one meetings. Remember, the absence of these characteristics is a red flag, not the presence of them.

**There will be temptation or doubt that they feel uncomfortable talking about**

It's common for there to be topics that a person gets weird about, and that doesn't always mean they are spiraling into that sin. They may have experienced temptation in that area and they feel ashamed, or many people will know that something is sin but since the world and progressive Christian circles affirm it they may be wrestling with their understanding.

Satan will plague people with guilt over temptation and doubt, even if they never act on it. It can be easy to feel like these thoughts that are pestering you are something to be ashamed of and, therefore, hidden. Sometimes our minds go places that we are afraid to admit to anyone, and we have to be aware that we are always only one bad decision away from committing any sin.

The problem with not telling anyone about temptation is that sin thrives and grows in isolation. When you think you are alone in the struggle of temptation, you are more likely to hide it out of shame, and Satan has a better chance to get you to sin in that exact way.

Isolating temptation or doubt can look like:
- Sudden change of demeanor when discussing a trigger subject
- Silence around a certain topic
- Vague answers that don't really address what was asked
- Muddled or skewed theology
- Acting nervous about asking a question

When you give sin time to fester or refuse to acknowledge it as a problem, it grows more powerful. But when you bring that sin or doubt or temptation to light, regardless of what it is, it diminishes. It loses its power, it loses its intensity, and it loses its hold over you.

Everyone has laundry they'd rather not air out. That might be because they feel that no one will understand or will lose respect for them. So as a Christian leader it is vital that you teach people the method for and importance of exposing sin. Galatians 5:11-13 says, *"Do not participate in the unfruitful deeds of darkness, but instead expose them; for it is disgraceful even to speak of the things which are done by them in secret. But all things become visible when they are exposed by the light, for everything that becomes visible is light."*

This is a normal impulse that many of the people in your congregation will be dealing with. Creating opportunities to address sin and training about how and why to bring sin/doubt/guilt/questions to light will help to nip future problems in the bud.

**They will have spiritual blind spots**

Another characteristic of a Christian with a normal sin nature is that they will have areas they just don't see in themselves. This is different than hiding a besetting sin or living in unrepentant sin.

A blind spot could be a tendency to gossip, get angry, or work for man's praise instead of God's. Things that are definitely sinful, but people don't tend to confront them. I have heard them called "acceptable sins" in the church, which is a phrase that turns my stomach.

A spiritual blind spot can look like:
- Turning to friends to talk out a problem and never praying about it
- Complaining about someone with no intention of fixing the issue
- Regular choices to put off responsibility in favor of leisure
- Holding grudges or taking up offence
- An attitude of pride and self-centeredness
- Angry outbursts or bitterness

I call these blind spots, not because they are lesser sins or not that big of a deal, but because it's hard to see them in yourself. When are you sharing with a friend and when are you gossiping? When is your anger justified and when is it too much? A person could go a long time without even noticing that they have a problem until someone points it out or God convicts them about it.

Another reason I like the term blind spot is that once the person becomes aware of this tendency, it is no longer a blind spot. When God has shown you your sin, you get to decide if you will obey or disobey him in dealing with it. Yes, it's hard to change a characteristic you've been building into a habit for years. Yes, it's annoying suddenly to have to stop yourself from doing something you haven't considered wrong. But being sanctified and growing to be more and more like Christ is all about this kind of work.

## There will be varying levels of spiritual maturity

In every Christian you interact with, you'll be able to see tangible evidence of their maturity in Christ. You'll see this in how they think through theological issues, where they invest their time, and how they respond to correction. God takes each of us on a journey of relationship with Him, so expect to see areas that have not yet been surrendered or concepts that haven't been worked through yet.

Someone's sin nature may still have habits worked into the framework of their life that they don't have the bandwidth to address yet. That is something we walk through with each other in fellowship and prayer that God will complete the work He started in each of us.

There will also always be issues that well-meaning and intelligent people understand differently, and unless they pervert the gospel, it is best to not continually argue about them (2 Timothy 2:14, 23-24). Be careful about creating discord within your church over things that are non-essential. Trust God to convict and lead His children into the truth.

Sanctification is a long and messy process, and it can be easy to get confused by all the different teachings and verses about what Christians should look like. We ARE sinners, and we need to equip our congregations and families to deal with their sin nature. However, praise God, we have been given everything we need for life and godliness, (2 Peter 1) and where we are weak we can rejoice because God's power is made perfect in weakness (2

Corinthians 12). There is grace to cover where we fall short, but we have a responsibility to not take that grace lightly. Romans 6 starts out with *"shall we go on sinning that grace may increase? By no means!"*

Skip one chapter over into Romans 7 and Paul is saying *"For I have the desire to do what is right, but not the ability to carry it out."* You will see this in people as you talk with them, a deep desire to do what is right but a complete loss as to the practical steps to change their own behavior. Their sin is a tangible thing to them, but the path to freedom seems vague and hard to comprehend. You have to show people, not just TELL them, but SHOW them that the frustrating struggle with sin is normal. But don't leave them there without hope. Just like it's easier to continue in sin after you have done it once, it's easier to confess and repent when you build that pattern into your life. You need to exercise the muscle of obedience, and in time you'll start to notice that muscle memory kicks in and it takes less of a battle to obey the next time.

✝

One thing I remember from my years of double-mindedness as a teenager is that all of my leaders loved me. I was told regularly that I was a model member of the youth group, even to the point that parents approached me asking if I would hang out with their daughters because they thought I was a good influence. A friend of mine remembers being in youth group and having multiple leaders say they wish they could just clone her.

This happens all over the church. If you stop right now and think of your congregation, I bet you could pick out a few who seem to be the cream of the crop. What is wrong with telling them so?

Imagine being a 15 year old who spends hours chatting with strangers online and describing in disgusting detail all of the lewd things they fantasize about. That same teenager goes to church, follows the rules, memorizes the verses, and gets told that the leaders wish the group was full of kids just like them.

No way that kid is telling anyone about their sin.

Here's a different scenario. Imagine being an elder in the church; you have a wife and three kids who are all following the Lord and you are often told how much people admire your strong leadership of your family. You smile and thank them, but you know that your family toes the line because you enforce how you expect them to behave with harshness. If anyone heard the way you speak to your wife and children, they might accuse you of abuse and your reputation would be shot.

But there's this barrier of perception that has been built up by the praise and subsequent expectations of people who didn't know they were harming instead of helping.

Paul rebukes the Corinthian church about putting leaders on a pedestal in 1 Corinthians 3, *"For when one says, "I follow Paul," and another, "I follow Apollos," are you not mere human beings? What, after all, is Apollos? And what is Paul? Only servants, through whom you came to believe—as the Lord has assigned to each his task."*

Putting people on a pedestal isolates them. And as I said before, sin *thrives* in isolation. When you layer on praise, it can be easy to give people an incorrect view of themselves. Someone might take that praise and be devastated on the inside because they will never measure up, and someone else might use that praise to layer the jewels on their self-created imaginary crown.

A correct view of yourself is vital to having a healthy relationship with God and the body of Christ. And part of facilitating that correct view is understanding that we all sin.

Not in a vague way. We all sin specifically.

The devastated teen needs to know that we all sin. Your sin does not diminish your value. Jesus died for each ugly thought. And there is non-judgmental help for you if you only ask.

The abusive elder needs to know that we all sin. Your violent words and actions are not excused because you think they deserve them. God is asking *you* for *your* obedience. And the only way to stop the escalation of your sin is to deal with it.

Putting people on a pedestal dehumanizes them. It creates in them a fear of falling. And we live in a fallen world, we all belong firmly on the ground, for we all have fallen short of the glory of God (Romans 3:23). Even our pastors, even our leaders, even the proverbial cream of the crop. When you learn to expect that humans have wicked, rotten hearts and desperately need the grace of God, then confessing sin isn't such a huge roadblock.

Your job is to show them how it's done. Show them that confession is a normal part of Christian life, just like a housekeeping task. It's a maintenance job. Remember, pretending to be without sin is like pretending that you don't ever use the toilet. Just kind of ridiculous. We all do it, and if we didn't, we'd get sick and die. So approach confession like the bathroom, you go in and get rid of the waste so your body can continue functioning properly. We all sin and need to confess for a clean conscience and healthy spiritual life.

Get off of your own pedestal and start revealing your humanity. Go first. I dare you to do it, and see who follows you.

# Reflect & Check

*Take a few minutes to pray about and answer these questions. Is God asking you to change, repent, or act differently as a leader or as a Christian?*

———

*Think of three specific Christian people that you know well. Do you see the evidence of a sin nature in them?*

*Who are the people in your church or family that are put on a pedestal? How can you help them down?*

*Ask God to show you how you can go first, and write down what He says.*

# Chapter Four

# Recognizing a Secret Sinner

*"...having the appearance of godliness,*
*but denying its power."*
*- 2 Timothy 3:5*

This is the chapter you've been waiting for. It's the one I am most anxious to write, because I know that those trapped in secret sin are a deceptive bunch. The Father of lies himself has taught them his craft, and they'll do nearly anything to avoid being found out.

But as a former secret sinner, I'd like to give you an inside view.

In the depths of their hearts where the Holy Spirit is incessantly pleading with them to surrender, they are longing for freedom. They are longing for rest.

To someone who is saved by the blood of Christ and also floundering in a pit of sin, the years stretching out ahead overwhelm them. I remember thinking, can I keep this up for years? Can I live with myself like this for decades? Constant emotional upheaval, repulsion at the escalating depravity of your own lust, and the never-ending fear of exposure. Could you do that for decades?

Charles Spurgeon, in his 1859 sermon titled A Divided Heart puts it this way: *"Men who are neither this nor that, neither one thing nor another, are always uneasy and miserable. The fear of discovery, and the consciousness of being wrong, conspire together to agitate the soul and make it full of unease, disease, and restlessness of spirit. Such a man is unhappy in himself."* [5]

There are many verses that speak about being double-minded, having a double heart or a divided heart (James 1:8, 4:8, Psalm 12:2, 86:11, 119:113, Hosea 10:2, Ezekiel 11:19, Matthew 6:24). The visual that is clearest to me is in Isaiah 29:13 (NASB), *"this people draw near with their words and honor me with their lip service, but they remove their hearts far from me."*

A divided/double heart and mind are exactly what is going on for a secret sinner. They have both the living Spirit of God and a gigantic stronghold of Satan within them. They are exhausted, and yet continually running scared from the peace that God offers through faith and obedience.

The Bible addresses strongholds in 2 Corinthians 10:4-5, *"The weapons we fight with are not the weapons of the world. On the contrary, they have divine power to demolish strongholds. We demolish arguments and every pretension that sets itself up against the knowledge of God, and we take captive every thought to make it obedient to Christ."*

Ed Silvoso says this, *"A spiritual stronghold is a mind-set impregnated with hopelessness that causes us to accept as unchangeable, situations that we know are contrary to the will of God."* [6]

Strongholds are found in your mind, and you can recognize them when you believe two completely contradictory things. For example, you know confession brings freedom, but you can't even visualize what that would look like. You know God is asking you to step out in faith in a certain area, but fear of the unknown has you crippled and shaking in your boots. God gives us weapons to tear these false beliefs down, and those weapons are the Word and prayer. But those weapons are only effective when you recognize the stronghold and declare war on it.

✚

For a Christian living in unrepentant sin, there is a cycle that occurs regularly. You give in to temptation and indulge your lust, and then when the high fades off you feel waves of disgust and self-loathing. The thought of whatever activity you just engaged in will repulse you. You'll fall on your face before God begging for forgiveness and asking him to change you, heal you, deliver you… you'll feel better, go about your life, and walk into temptation again.

The cycle is always always just between you and God; in fact, you might have tried a time or two to barter with him, "I'll do XYZ as long as we can keep this just between us." Confessing your sin to another human seems impossible, but there's no danger in confessing to God because you can't hide it from Him anyway.

This is why we are instructed to confess our sins *to one another* in James 5. It goes on to say confess and *"pray for one another that you may be healed. The prayer of a righteous man is powerful and effective."*

The title of this book is taken from Joel 2:13. I've always been struck by this statement because I can see the sin/confess cycle so clearly here.

In the Old Testament you see many instances of people wearing sackcloth and ashes or tearing their clothes as a sign of repentance (2 Samuel 3:31, Genesis 37:34, Esther 4:1, Jonah 3:5-7, Isaiah 37:1, 2 Kings 19:2, Lamentations 2:10, Daniel 9:3). But Joel is speaking to Israel at a time when they were not following God at all, and any of the rituals they were still holding to were empty because their hearts were far from repentant for their sins. Joel writes striking visuals of God's coming wrath, and then pleads with them to turn and repent. *"Even now... return to me with all your heart, with fasting and weeping and mourning. Rend your heart and not your garments. Return to the Lord your God... who knows? He may turn and relent."* Joel 2:12-14

When I rip my clothes and wail, I present a visual and dramatic display of repentance before God, I might *feel* very sorry for what I did. I'm certainly acting very sorry. But the power to break chains is not in a momentary public display of sorrow. The power to break chains is in the Holy Spirit transforming a heart that is obedient and submissive to His work. God isn't asking for torn clothes or sackcloth and ashes. He's asking for a torn heart.

I often think of this outward appearance of repentance when I hear people say, as I have often said before, that they are struggling with sin. We like to say that phrase, implying that we're doing our best to overpower the sin nature and force ourselves into obedience to God. But I think most of the time that's a phrase we use to feel better about what is really going on.

One of my favorite authors and theologians is Elisabeth Elliot. Her insights into living a life of daily obedience have shaped me in many ways. She says, *"If we examine our consciences deliberately, clearly, and in the presence of God, I think we're going to find out that a whole lot of what we call "struggling" is delayed obedience."* [7] I know that in my situation, the Spirit was prompting me to act, to obey God by confessing my sin, and I chose deliberately not to. I was not struggling against my sinful habits, I was struggling against obeying God's prompting to confess and repent. What I called "struggling with sin" was actually struggling with God.

I wasn't fighting Satan, I was on his side. Both Satan and I wanted my sin to remain hidden and unaddressed. God was the only one fighting for my freedom from bondage.

Obedience is not a vague concept, though we teach it that way at times. When God asks us to obey Him, He makes it clear to us what we are supposed to do. He asks us to obey Him by forgiving others, by giving of ourselves, by sacrifice, and by suffering. He asks us to obey Him in sharing the gospel, in standing in the truth, and in confessing our sin. Paul writes in Acts 26:20, *"I preached that they should repent and turn to God and demonstrate their repentance by their deeds."* and in 1 Corinthians 7:10, *"Godly sorrow brings repentance that leads to salvation and leaves no regret, but worldly sorrow brings death."*

If you sit in silence and let Him speak, you'll know what He is asking you to do specifically. Just obey Him. If you can't choose obedience, you'll circle the sin/confess cycle forever. True repentance is obedience to God with a broken heart.

✝

Satan has been carefully cultivating sexual sin in the hearts of Christians for years, and it has permeated the church. The stories of Christian leaders being exposed after years of abusing their power are absolutely horrifying. If sexual perversion is so prevalent in the leadership of the church, just imagine how many men, women, and children in the congregation have to be trapped in sexual sin as well.

As each name hits the spotlight and crashes from public esteem, I see the reactions as people ask how such a good and godly man or woman could have been hiding a sin like that. So I'd like to paint a picture for you of how that could have happened.

There once was a little boy named Jack who grew up in a Christian home and went to church twice a week. Jack was taught that lust and pornography and sex outside of marriage were wrong. This was emphasized to him as a teenager specifically. But beyond saying that those things are wrong, his family and his church did not teach much about how to deal with temptation other than telling him to flee it. They assumed that his sense of morality and the Holy Spirit's conviction would keep him from sexual sin. Without any practical tools though, he soon found himself discovering how good it felt to touch himself, or the effect on his body when he let himself look at the magazine rack at the grocery store or women around him.

Jack's interest in sex grew as he let his eyes and his mind wander, and eventually he found ways to access pornography. He felt ashamed after engaging in porn or masturbation, but quickly turned his mind elsewhere. As he considered his chosen path of ministry, Jack pushed his sexual habits to the back of his mind, only letting them out when he was alone in secret and dark places. He grew up and started rising in leadership, moving from position to position and mentor to mentor who never asked him the questions that need to be asked.

He started dating a good Christian girl and married her, thinking that this would end his sexual temptation. But by that point he had created a habit and expectation of sex that couldn't be fulfilled in a monogamous relationship. His porn use continued, and his conscience was riddled with guilt. But slowly, as the years went by, his conscience became seared over and numb to the Holy Spirit's prompting.

After 20 years in ministry, Jack was offered a position of power and influence where everyone was looking to him for spiritual guidance. And suddenly, the work that Satan had been doing in him since childhood had space to grow. He had freedom to make his own hours, to spend huge chunks of time alone in prayer and study. No one was questioning or accusing him. Those hours in his office with unfiltered access to the internet took his porn use to levels of depravity that would have shocked him just a few years prior.

The enemy pulled him down a wide path that gently descended into darkness. His pornography wasn't doing it for him anymore and he started to notice the shapely bodies of the young people in his congregation. Young people who may need his wisdom and mentorship.

He was misunderstood. He had needs. He had justified his sin for so long that it wasn't any trouble to switch from masking pornography to masking abuse. Years of lies had given him a silver tongue to convince whoever was in his way. He had reason to be alone with his victims and power over anyone who might talk.

This story, or a variation of it, happens all over the world. It isn't something that only happens to pastors, it happens to men and women in every walk of life.

The fact that his family and church did not address sin and temptation very thoroughly does not make Jack's actions less sinful. His sin is his fault and his responsibility. It is a natural progression of a depraved heart. He made the choices that resulted in the man he became.

The question for us is, how can we prevent this story from repeating, unchecked, in the lives of our sons and daughters?

What if, in addition to teaching him that sexual sin is wrong, his family and church provided opportunities for confession and accountability? What if there was regular training and teaching about how to combat sin? What if his mentor or his parents asked him directly if he struggled with pornography or shared their personal sin struggles and asked if they could pray together for the Spirit to reveal sin in their hearts? What if he knew spiritually mature men who practiced confession and talked about what living in freedom looked like for them? What if the church or organization he worked for implemented safeguards to protect him against sin? What if there were men around him regularly praying together, confronting sin in each other, and spurring one another on toward love and good works?

Would his story have been different? I don't know. Maybe he would have made the same choices. But as a Christian leader, I challenge you to think about your church or ministry or family and ask yourself if there are tools and safeguards in place to keep people from getting to this point.

Stop right now and think of a young boy or girl in your church, around 12 or 13 years old. Think of them by name. What if this child that you are thinking of was addicted to pornography right now? What should she do? Who should he talk to? Has your church given her the tools to find help? Are they readily available, and is he seeing examples of men and women who are using those avenues of confession and accountability?

How should she confront her sin?

If you don't know, you have to see that she doesn't know either.

✚

As a secret sinner rises to influence within the church, they can become more and more blind to the hypocrisy in their own life. They perfect the art of lying to themselves, to the point that they can feel genuine when they give advice to others. They might counsel someone in the very sin they are trapped in without batting an eye.

This is a perfect example of double-mindedness, or *"holding at the same time mutually exclusive beliefs"* [8] as Pastor Jim Reed puts it in his sermon *Destroying Strongholds.* It is very difficult to go through life holding onto a mindset that our situation will never change while also knowing the truth that our God can do all things. What we end up doing is building walls that compartmentalize these beliefs, so we don't have to deal with seeing that truth of God's goodness and holiness while living in the lie that they aren't strong enough to change our hearts or circumstances.

In Matthew 23:25-26 Jesus condemns the Pharisees, *"Woe to you, scribes and Pharisees, hypocrites! For you clean the outside of the cup and the plate, but inside they are full of greed and self-indulgence. You blind Pharisee! First clean the inside of the cup and the plate, that the outside also may be clean."*

Satan's goal is to get you to the point where you are fully convinced of your own righteousness. Where you've built those walls of double-mindedness so high that it is easy for you to pretend as if the sin in your life doesn't matter and wear a mask of self-righteousness. He doesn't want you to agonize over each choice, he wants you to gloss over all the sin that is festering and rotting inside.

When someone is at the point that they would say "of course, God has called us to deny ourselves and follow him" but never let it occur to them that this means they should deny their fleshly desires, Satan wins.

James 1:22-24 addresses in this by saying, *"But be doers of the word, and not hearers only, deceiving yourselves. For if anyone is a hearer of the word and not a doer, he is like a man who looks intently at his natural face in a mirror. For he looks at himself and goes away and at once forgets what he was like."* (ESV)

The cause of evil is never more secure in a Christian's heart than when they can look at themselves squarely in the face, know the sin they are allowing to run rampant in their life, and walk away, immediately pushing it from their mind.

There is zero intent to obey. Even in a sinner who cycles into false repentance periodically, there is no real intent to obey.

I want to address another kind of sin. We have talked about the secret sin hidden carefully away in a Christian's heart. We have talked about "acceptable" sins that you mostly overlook because they start out subtly and you don't notice the slow increase in your life and church. But there is another way Satan encourages us to sin and in my mind, it's the most dangerous.

Since the beginning we've been twisting God's words and commands to have a meaning we find more favorable. The serpent did this with Eve in Genesis 3, Paul and Peter both teach about this in the New Testament (2 Timothy 4:3-4, Romans 16:17-20, 2 Peter 3:16, 2 Corinthians 11:14-15). It's not a new practice. But I see some churches softening their approach to these topics and even embracing them instead of calling them out as sin and false teaching.

When Christians justify their sin to the point of not feeling the need to hide it anymore and when they band together with like-minded people to create an interpretation of scripture that supports their opinion, Satan has won an army that will do his work of deception for him.

No one will argue more passionately to bring people over to their way of thinking than a Christian defending their shady theology. No one will avoid and condemn people who point out the holes in their logic like a Christian who is desperate to justify their sin. They surround themselves with others who agree with them and recruit other immature believers who are easily swayed.

My heart breaks even when writing this, because only the Holy Spirit can get through the stone walls of reasoning they've set up between their heart and the truth of scripture. If you know that I'm talking about you, I'd ask you to do one thing before you dismiss what I am saying. Re-study and reconsider your position, begging God for insight, and resolve to obey Him no matter what He reveals to you.

The warnings in the New Testament are about someone. Read them with a heart to listen. Ask God if they are about you.

*"For the time is coming when people will not endure sound teaching, but having itching ears they will accumulate for themselves teachers to suit their own passions, and will turn away from listening to the truth and wander off into myths."* 2 Timothy 4:3-4

*"I appeal to you, brothers, to watch out for those who cause divisions and create obstacles contrary to the doctrine that you have been taught; avoid them. For such persons do not serve our Lord*

*Christ, but their own appetites, and by smooth talk and flattery they deceive the hearts of the naive. For your obedience is known to all, so that I rejoice over you, but I want you to be wise as to what is good and innocent as to what is evil. The God of peace will soon crush Satan under your feet. The grace of our Lord Jesus Christ be with you."*
Romans 16:17-20

*"And no wonder, for even Satan disguises himself as an angel of light. So it is no surprise if his servants, also, disguise themselves as servants of righteousness. Their end will correspond to their deeds."* 2 Corinthians 11:14-15

*"As he does in all his letters when he speaks in them of these matters. There are some things in them that are hard to understand, which the ignorant and unstable twist to their own destruction, as they do the other Scriptures."* 2 Peter 3:16

Paul warns in 2 Timothy 3 about what people will be like in the last days. I remember reading these verses as a teenager and feeling cut to my core. *"[People will be] lovers of pleasure rather than*

*lovers of God, having the appearance of godliness,
but denying its power. Avoid such people. For
among them are those who creep into households
and capture weak women, burdened with sins and
led astray by various passions, always learning and
never able to arrive at a knowledge of the truth."*

I couldn't decide if I was the person with the
appearance of godliness who denied the power of
godliness because I was so corrupted, or if I was
the weak willed woman burdened with sin. What
haunted me was that phrase, *"always learning and
never able to arrive at a knowledge of the truth."*

It's a bleak future.

In a way I was probably both. I was a weak woman,
burdened with sin and led astray by passions that I
wasn't able to control. I was always learning, in
church being mentored and discipled, but never
able to grasp whatever the magic bullet was that
would help me get free from my compulsions.
Never arriving at a real knowledge of the truth that
could set people free. In the same breath, I was a
lover of pleasure rather than a lover of God. I
appeared godly on the outside, but I had none of

the power that real godliness brings with it naturally.

Every sinner is faced with a choice. Not between choosing God or sin, because they have already chosen sin, but they are faced with the choice to keep going or turn back. They are on a road to Hell. People you talk to every week, people you love, maybe even people you look up to.

To this sinner, this lost soul that seems past all hope, God is calling. He is pleading with them to come back. He is saying, *"I will remove from you your heart of stone and give you a heart of flesh."* (Ezekiel 36:26) He is offering to pull them from the mire and place their feet back on solid ground. They just have to take it.

It's not too late, and you aren't too far gone.

# Reflect & Check

*Take a few minutes to pray about and answer these questions. Is God asking you to change, repent, or act differently as a leader or as a Christian?*

———

*Are you a secret sinner?*

*What does the sin/confess cycle of false repentance look like in your life?*

*Ask God to search your heart and reveal your sin and write down what He says.*

*Chapter Five*
# The Father of Lies

*"The thief comes only to steal and kill and destroy. I
came that they may have life and have it abundantly."
- John 10:10*

The worst cop-out in the history of the world is an
old classic: "The devil made me do it." We have a
warped perception and lazy theology when it
comes to Satan's role in our lives, using him as a
convenient way to pass the buck when it comes to
being holy.

Remember the part where you have your very own
personalized sin nature? The devil does not make
you wretched and depraved. You're pretty good at
that on your own. If you believe that Satan's
interference in your life is the only thing that keeps
you from God, you'd be wrong. Even without him,
your sin nature separates you from God
completely.

At the same time, Satan sucks. He hates God, he
hates us, and he is never happier than when we

are tangled up in sin and completely ineffective. He is described as a schemer (Ephesians 6:11), a cunning deceiver (2 Corinthians 11:3), a murderer and a liar (John 8:44), a thief (John 10:10), your enemy (1 Peter 5:8), an accuser (Revelation 12:10), and a tempter (Matthew 4).

I believe that Satan is an opportunist.

He prowls, he roams, looking for opportunity to sin and provoke sin. 1 John 3:8 says, *"The one who does what is sinful is of the devil, because the devil has been sinning from the beginning. The reason the Son of God appeared was to destroy the devil's work."*

For me, that opportunity was my 8 year old self looking at that magazine by the creek. It was an opportunity to get a foothold in an area of my life, and one that he has been very successful with with many many people before me. So he took that opportunity and won 10 years of my slavery to sin.

A friend of mine aptly said that Satan is a button-pusher. He knows where we are weak and he applies pressure there. I have a theory that we each have a tendency toward certain types of sin, which is why you might see one person who has a huge pride problem but has never struggled with an addiction, or someone crippled by sloth and gluttony who is serving God in other areas. Satan sees our natural weakness and he capitalizes on it.

Amy Carmichael, the Christian missionary who served orphans in India for 55 years without furlough wrote this: *"Satan is so much more in earnest than we are--he buys up the opportunity while we are wondering how much it will cost."* [9]

His power is limited; remember, he was an angel, not a deity. So he can't be in more than one place at a time. He can't know your thoughts. But I'm sure a few thousand years of observation have given him some good insight into human nature.

One of my favorite books is *The Screwtape Letters* by C.S. Lewis; it is written as a series of letters from the demon Screwtape to his nephew Wormwood, who is a novice demon in his first assignment to secure the damnation of a human. The letters revealed to me all of the ways that my boredom, discontent, frustration, fantasy, and pride keep me from being effective and obedient in this life.

*"It does not matter how small the sins are provided that their cumulative effect is to edge the man away from the Light and out into the Nothing. Murder is no better than cards if cards can do the trick. Indeed the safest road to Hell is the gradual one--the gentle slope, soft underfoot, without sudden turnings, without milestones, without signposts."* [10] *(The Screwtape Letters, C.S. Lewis)*

So if Satan can't be in every ear at once, maybe he does have demons assigned to us to whisper suggestions of self-indulgence, skepticism, and shame in our ears.

Satan and his demons are liars, and some of their favorite lies (at least the lies they told me) were that I was alone, that no one would understand, and if anyone knew the truth about me, I would lose all of the respect of everyone I cared about.

Paul tells us in Ephesians 6 that we need the full armor of God *so that we can* stand firm against the schemes of the devil. Without the protection of the armor (which is made up of truth, righteousness, the gospel of peace, faith, salvation, and the word of God), we are so vulnerable to his schemes. Like a soldier jumping onto the front lines without a helmet or bulletproof vest or a weapon, we are fools if we think we can navigate life without building up methods of attack and defense against the devil.

**Truth defends us against Satan's lies.** When you read the Bible consistently, you will know the truth about God, His will, and His purposes for us. Then the lies that the devil tells you will stand out as false. *"Do your best to present yourself to God as one approved, a worker who has no need to be ashamed, rightly handling the word of truth."* 2 Timothy 2:15

**Righteousness defends us against Satan's accusations.** Not righteousness in our own merit or by our works, but the gift of righteousness freely given to us by Christ. *"how much more will those who receive God's abundant provision of grace and of the gift of righteousness reign in life through the one man, Jesus Christ!"* Romans 5:17b

**Peace defends us from Satan's scare tactics.** The good news of peace is that these troubles and threats dim in the light of eternity. We have security because we serve a God who never fails. *"Peace I leave with you, My peace I give to you; not as the world gives do I give to you. Let not your heart be troubled, neither let it be afraid."* John 14:27

**Faith defends us against Satan's direct attacks, his flaming arrows or fiery darts.** Most commentators define these as temptations to sin, and the shield of faith in Jesus Christ allows us not only to be protected from the flaming arrows, but *extinguish* them. *"In addition to all this, take up the shield of faith, with which you can extinguish all the flaming arrows of the evil one."* Ephesians 6:16

**Salvation defends us from Satan's goal.** He is a murderer. He wants us dead, forever separated from God and glory, like he is. And the helmet of salvation thwarts that purpose. We are saved through Christ, and we cling to that when the devil attacks. *"Therefore he is able to save completely those who come to God through him, because he always lives to intercede for them."* Hebrews 7:25

**The Sword of the Spirit, which is the Word of God, is our offensive weapon.** Charles Spurgeon in his sermon The Sword of the Spirit had this to say, *"But Paul, for excellent reasons, concentrates* *our offensive weapon in one, because it answers for all. We are to use the sword, and that only. Therefore, if you are going to this fight, see well to your only weapon. If you are to have no other, take care that you have this always in your hand. Let the Captain's voice ring in your ear, "Take the sword! Take the sword!", and so go forth to the field."* [11]

As I pointed out before, the armor of God is followed immediately by a call to prayer. In the ESV and ASV versions they don't even put a period after the instruction to take up the sword. The text flows into a call to prayer, supplication, and remaining alert.

For a Christian, Satan's aim is to make us as ineffective as possible. He is very very good at rendering us useless for kingdom building by keeping us focused on the temporal things of this world.

When you are caught up in drama within the Body of Christ. When you are refusing to throw off the sin that is entangling you. When you are unwilling to put in the work that it takes to grow to spiritual

94

maturity, that's when you bench yourself. Peter writes this: *"...make every effort to add to your faith goodness; and to goodness, knowledge; and to knowledge, self-control; and to self-control, perseverance; and to perseverance, godliness; and to godliness, mutual affection; and to mutual affection, love. For if you possess these qualities in increasing measure, they will keep you from being ineffective and unproductive in your knowledge of our Lord Jesus Christ. But whoever does not have them is nearsighted and blind, forgetting that they have been cleansed from their past sins."* 2 Peter 1:5-9

Regardless of if you believe salvation can be lost or not, the Bible makes it clear that those who once believed but turn away from the truth are doing the unthinkable. Nothing is playing into Satan's hands more than taking a child of God, created in His image, fully loved by the Creator, and slowly conditioning them to choose to walk away. Some of the passages that scared and convicted me the most when I was choosing sin were:

*"You are the salt of the earth. But if the salt loses its saltiness, how can it be made salty again? It is no*

*longer good for anything, except to be thrown out and trampled by men."* Matthew 5:13

*"It is for freedom that Christ has set us free. Stand firm, then, and do not let yourselves be burdened again by a yoke of slavery."* Galatians 5:1

*"If they have escaped the corruption of the world by knowing our Lord and Savior Jesus Christ and are again entangled in it and are overcome, they are worse off at the end than they were at the beginning. It would have been better for them not to have known the way of righteousness, than to have known it and then to turn their backs on the sacred command that was passed on to them."* 2 Peter 2:20-21

*"For if we go on sinning deliberately after receiving the knowledge of the truth, there no longer remains a sacrifice for sins, but a fearful expectation of judgment, and a fury of fire that will consume the adversaries. Anyone who rejected the law of Moses died without mercy on the testimony of two or three witnesses. How much more severely do you think someone deserves to be punished who has trampled the Son of God underfoot, who has treated as an unholy thing the blood of the*

*covenant that sanctified them, and who has insulted the Spirit of grace?"* Hebrews 10:26-29

*"No one who abides in him keeps on sinning; no one who keeps on sinning has either seen him or known him."* 1 John 3:6

*"Whoever believes in the Son has eternal life; whoever does not obey the Son shall not see life, but the wrath of God remains on him."* John 3:36

*"For it is impossible, in the case of those who have once been enlightened, who have tasted the heavenly gift, and have shared in the Holy Spirit, and have tasted the goodness of the word of God and the powers of the age to come, and then have fallen away, to restore them again to repentance, since they are crucifying once again the Son of God to their own harm and holding him up to contempt."* Hebrews 6:4-6

Read through these verses with the knowledge that, in light of eternity, we don't get to decide what they mean. God is the one who knows where the line is between saved and not. But ask yourself, is there unrepentant, deliberate sin in your life? Are you taking sin seriously when you confront it in others? How are you aware of and derailing Satan's efforts to make these verses a reality for you and your loved ones?

✝

Our enemy is very knowledgeable. He has resources and tactics to snare us and pull us out of our resolve to obey God. But we have resources too! In 1 John 4:4 we read that the one who is in us is greater than he that is in the world. God gives us defenses, a weapon, and a call to resist the enemy's advances.

RESIST. That's what he asks of us. Not to battle on our own, not to find the strength to face a beast, but to resist. And resist doesn't mean stand still with your eyes shut and will the temptation away. You have weapons, so fight back! Don't go willingly. Use the resources he gave you: the Bible, prayer, the church, mentors, fasting, and more besides.

Training and disciplining yourself spiritually isn't just for spiritual fitness, like a bodybuilder trains just for competition. It's for battle. Your spiritual fitness will be tested in spiritual warfare for your soul and the souls of those around you.

*"Be alert and of sober mind. Your enemy the devil prowls around like a roaring lion looking for someone to devour. Resist him, standing firm in the faith, because you know that the family of believers throughout the world is undergoing the same kind of sufferings."* 1 Peter 5:8-9

*"Submit yourselves, then, to God. Resist the devil, and he will flee from you."* James 4:7

# Reflect & Check

*Take a few minutes to pray about and answer these questions. Is God asking you to change, repent, or act differently as a leader or as a Christian?*

———

*What are your weak areas? What buttons are the easiest for Satan to push and tempt you to sin?*

*What opportunities has Satan taken advantage of in your past?*

*Ask God to show you a specific tool you can use to resist Satan and your sin nature, and write down what He says.*

*Chapter Six*

# Coming to the
# End of Yourself

*"When Jesus saw him lying there and learned that he
had been in this condition for a long time, he asked him,
'Do you want to get well?'"*
*- John 5:6*

One of Jesus' miracles occurred by the pool of
Bethesda in Jerusalem. John writes that a large
number of disabled people, blind, lame, and
paralyzed, would come and lie by this pool. Some
Biblical manuscripts include an explanation for why
they did so: *"..they waited for the moving of the
waters. From time to time an angel of the Lord
would come down and stir up the waters. The first
one into the pool after each such disturbance would
be cured of whatever disease they had."* John 5:4

When Jesus entered the city that day there was a
man lying by the pool who had been sick for 38
years. Jesus saw him, learned that he had been

sick a long time, and asked him, "Do you want to get well?"

I've read articles and heard sermons comment on how strange it was to ask that question. Of course! He had been sick for 38 years! Of course he wanted to be well!

But I have never thought that question was strange.

Humans can adapt to situations. We get used to things as they are. We can weather awful conditions for a very long time, and after awhile, they start to feel normal. Even comfortable. We know the routine of being ill. We are used to dismissing the feelings of guilt as we carry on in sin, conveniently ignoring the Spirit's conviction.

When Jesus asked if he wanted to be well, I can imagine the man's first reaction was shock and disbelief. His response was defensive--an explanation of why he hadn't been able to get down to the water for healing. And I understand how he felt, because, in my mind, getting well is a lot of responsibility.

Getting well physically requires discomfort, learning to use the muscles that have atrophied, energy--both physical and mental--humility, and courage. It means being vulnerable. It means having people all up in your business as you recover and figure out how to navigate the world like a healthy human being. It's not easy.

Coming to the point where you are really willing to deal with your sin 100% is similar.

Dealing with sin also requires discomfort, unlearning the sinful habits we are accustomed to, learning new habits to take their place, physical, emotional, and mental energy, vulnerability, humility, and courage. In many cases it means letting people get all up in your business. It's not fun. It's *wayyyyyy* easier to stay sick, both physically and spiritually.

Jesus asks us, "Do you want to get well?"

Eh, I don't know.

We may wish that we wanted to. But sometimes we just don't. Not really. We don't hate our sin enough to face it head on with the conviction that a life of holiness is worth what it will cost us.

We don't really hate our sin at all. We've diluted the term and created a vagueness around the concept, so we don't feel the harsh reality of the word that means we are choosing to cheat on our savior.

Jeremiah 2:20, 23-25 gives us another picture of Israel as a faithless wife: *"Indeed, on every high hill and under every spreading tree you lay down as a prostitute… You are a swift she-camel running here and there, a wild donkey accustomed to the desert, sniffing the wind in her craving— in her heat who can restrain her? Any males that pursue her need not tire themselves; at mating time they will find her. But you said, 'It's no use! I love foreign gods, and I must go after them.'"*

When you refuse to deal with your sin, you are telling God, "It's no use! I love my sin and I won't give it up." It doesn't seem so bad when your sin is gossip, but look at it from this perspective. God is saying, "Stop sowing seeds of contention into my church. Use your words and your energy and your time to build up the people around you rather than tear them down." And your answer? Sorry, Lord. I love the thrill of a juicy story more than I love you.

*Come back to me.*

No.

*Obey me.*

It's no use.

No one is paying the adulterous wife to be their whore, she is literally throwing her husband's gifts in front of them and begging them to come to her bed. Her lust is insatiable. The ugly fascination and trance of sin over her life is causing her to be aroused by the depraved, the disgusting, the warped, the unnatural. That's what sin does to our minds.

Later, in Jeremiah 2:33, God speaks to her, *"How skilled you are at pursuing love! Even the worst of women can learn from your ways."*

What a terrible skill. To have honed and practiced your sin until you excel at pursuing love outside of the covenant you entered into with your Lord.

You don't want to get well. Not enough.

And so, what other choice does God have? He has to discipline us. He loves us too much to let us continue in our sin, he knows that the consequences could be eternal. Like a parent who, out of love, punishes their child to teach them the consequences of poor choices, our God disciplines us out of love.

*"Endure hardship as discipline; God is treating you as his children. For what children are not disciplined by their father? If you are not disciplined—and everyone undergoes discipline—then you are not legitimate, not true sons and daughters at all. Moreover, we have all had human fathers who disciplined us and we respected them for it. How much more should we submit to the Father of spirits and live! They disciplined us for a little while as they thought best; but God disciplines us for our good, in order that we may share in his holiness. No discipline seems pleasant at the time, but painful. Later on, however, it produces a harvest of righteousness and peace for those who have been trained by it."*

Hebrews 12:7-11

Earlier in Hebrews we read a warning about how severely someone deserves to be punished who, after being saved, deliberately continues in sin. The writer continues: *"It is a dreadful thing to fall into the hands of the living God."* Hebrews 10:31. It is a dreadful thing. We should fear. A healthy and realistic fear of God's discipline. He will drive us to the end of ourselves and back into His arms.

For years, God sent prophets to warn Israel that their sin would not go unpunished, but they persisted in their disobedience, rebellion, and idolatry. He was clear. Repent and obey or face exile. Deuteronomy 29:24-28 is one passage of many that gives this warning:

*"...the nations will ask: "Why has the Lord done this to this land? Why this fierce, burning anger?" And the answer will be: "It is because this people abandoned the covenant of the Lord, the God of their ancestors, the covenant he made with them when he brought them out of Egypt. They went off and worshiped other gods and bowed down to them, gods they did not know, gods he had not*

*given them. Therefore the Lord's anger burned against this land, so that he brought on it all the curses written in this book. In furious anger and in great wrath the Lord uprooted them from their land and thrust them into another land, as it is now.""*

Exile. Being torn from the promised land and forced to live again under the oppression of their enemies. Israel's ancestors had been exiles in Egypt for 430 years, they knew their history. But they chose to continue in their sin against God.

Assyria took the northern part of the kingdom in 722BC, and in 586BC the Babylonians destroyed the temple and took the southern kingdom into exile.

In Ezekiel's prophecy about the adulterous bride, there is a point where God has had enough. He gathers her lovers and strips her naked before them, turning her over to their cruelty. Lamentations 1:8-9 also gives a vivid retelling of this:

*"Jerusalem has sinned greatly
    and so has become unclean.
All who honored her despise her,
    for they have all seen her naked;*

*she herself groans*
*and turns away.*
*Her filthiness clung to her skirts;*
*she did not consider her future.*
*Her fall was astounding;*
*there was none to comfort her."*

Tucked in the book of Jeremiah, you'll find a page
that recounts the story of the Rekabites. They don't
get very much recognition in Sunday School, but
God drew Jeremiah's attention to them and asked
him to invite the entire family to the temple and
offer them some wine.

Odd request, God.

When the Rekabites were offered wine to drink they
declined, saying that their forefather Jehonadab
son of Rekab had commanded that neither they nor
their descendants were to drink wine, build houses,
sow seeds, or plant vineyards. Rather they were to
live in tents like nomads. The entire line had
obeyed this command down to the last soul.

God said to Jeremiah, *"Jehonadab son of Rekab ordered his descendants not to drink wine and this command has been kept. To this day they do not drink wine, because they obey their forefather's command. But I have spoken to you again and again, yet you have not obeyed me."* Jeremiah 35:14.

God puts stock in obedience. In John 14:23 Jesus says *"Anyone who loves me will obey my teaching."* The Rekabites, though never mentioned again in scripture, are rewarded for their obedience with the promise that they would never lack a man to stand before Him.

There's another story in Matthew 19 of the rich man who isn't willing to give up his riches to follow Christ. When he walks away, Jesus turns to His disciples and says that it is easier for a camel to pass through the eye of a needle than for a rich man to enter the kingdom of heaven, but then He says that with God all things are possible.

We usually hear that phrase out of context, like "you might think you will never be successful, but with God all things are possible!", but what Jesus was saying right then was not that all success and glory is possible, but that all sacrifice and self-control is possible.  All heart wrenching pain to follow Christ is possible, all denying of the self is possible, all daily making the choice to obey and squash the flesh is possible.

He wasn't saying that God can fly you to the highest heights (which he can), but that God can pull you through the darkest depths.  That is the promise He is making here, and that is the promise that we desperately need.

But for Israel, time had run out. Disobedience caught up with them and exile had driven them to far off lands. Just like their forefathers in Egypt, they had many years of wilderness stretching out ahead.

The prophets during the exile have always struck a chord with me. The book of Lamentations is a poetic book, written in the years of Babylonian exile, and it expresses God's role as the disciplinarian in ways that I can understand. There is a point where He has to execute judgment out of love. Chapter 2 verse 5 starts out with, *"The Lord is like an enemy."*

*"He has driven and brought me*
*into darkness without any light;*
*surely against me he turns his hand*
*again and again the whole day long...*
*He has walled me about so that I cannot escape;*
*he has made my chains heavy;*
*though I call and cry for help,*
*he shuts out my prayer;*
*he has blocked my ways with blocks of stones;*
*he has made my paths crooked.*
*He is a bear lying in wait for me,*
*a lion in hiding;*
*he turned aside my steps and tore me to pieces;*
*he has made me desolate;*
*he bent his bow and set me*
*as a target for his arrow....*
*He has made my teeth grind on gravel,*
*and made me cower in ashes;*
*my soul is bereft of peace;*
*I have forgotten what happiness is;*
*so I say, "My endurance has perished;*
*so has my hope from the Lord."*

Lamentations 3:2-3, 7-12, 16-18


When I was living in sin I knew that my time was
coming. I was on edge waiting for God to turn on

me and expose my sin. He felt like an enemy, bent on the destruction and uprooting of life as I knew it. Determined to burn me to the ground to clean out the rot I was letting fester in my heart.

*"See, I will refine and test them, for what else can I do because of the sin of my people?"* Jeremiah 9:7

What choice does God have but to turn against us when we are determined to worship other gods and put our trust in the ways of the world? Remember He disciplines us out of love, with the goal of bringing us back into fellowship, so He isn't smiting us or wiping us off the face of the earth. He is systematically destroying the work of the devil as 1 John 3:8 says, *"The reason the Son of God appeared was to destroy the devil's work."*

The last time God wiped humanity off the face of the earth was in Genesis 6 with the great flood. Humanity had become corrupt and full of violence, so God decided to start over with Noah and his family.

At the end of that story in Genesis 9 God does an amazing thing. He gives Noah a sign and makes a covenant with him: *"Whenever I bring clouds over the earth and the rainbow appears in the clouds, I will remember my covenant between me and you and all living creatures of every kind. Never again will the waters become a flood to destroy all life. Whenever the rainbow appears in the clouds, I will see it and remember the everlasting covenant between God and all living creatures of every kind on the earth."* Genesis 9:14-16.

God gives Noah a clear sign of this covenant. And think of what this is costing God; He now has committed to these people no matter how vile they get. He marries Himself to them. He will not wipe them out again.

The rainbow is God's DTR (defining the relationship) talk with us. He is saying that He is committed to us 100%.

And so when humanity becomes corrupt and violent again? When we seek after idols and worship the desires of the flesh and reject our husbands for hookups with strange men? What choice does God have?

He needs to purge the sin. And it's going to hurt.

# Reflect & Check

*Take a few minutes to pray about and answer these questions. Is God asking you to change, repent, or act differently as a leader or as a Christian?*

———

*Do you really want to be well?*

*Has God ever felt like an enemy to you?*

*Ask God to bring you to the end of yourself and write down what He says.*

*Chapter Seven*

# The Mercy of Discipline

*"Though he brings grief, he will show compassion, so
great is his unfailing love."*
*- Lamentations 3:32*

I hope you are tracking with me to this point. God
sees our sin in a much different way than we teach
in sanctuaries and classrooms across the world.
Sin is present in the heart of every believer, and we
need to expect to see the results of its presence.
Some of us are in over our heads, and secret sin is
consuming our lives. The devil encourages this, he
seeks out our weak spots and makes great effort to
trap us into a corner. And God loves us so much
that He refines and tests and ravages us in an
effort to turn our hearts from the sin that we are
choosing.

One thing that I have come to understand about my
own heart is that I yearn to be both fully known and
fully loved.

I know that my heart is wicked. The depths of my own depravity scare me frequently. But all I have ever wanted, from a friend, from my husband, from my family, from my God, is to look into the eyes of someone who knows the worst of me and loves me in spite of it.

Without being fully known, you will always doubt that you are fully loved.

This is our God, friends. He is not surprised by our sin. He will not tolerate it. And through Jesus' blood He looks beyond it to see the child that He created and loved. He knows us fully and He loves us fully.

I think of the story of Jesus leaving the 99 sheep to come back for the one. We often think of that as Him caring for us individually, which is true. But I think we need to realize that we need Jesus to come back for us because of how far short we fall of His standard. It isn't because we're a cute innocent lamb who got lost. He comes back for us in our deepest shame and pain and rebellion. And so many times that act of love when we are at our lowest is what pushes us over the edge to true repentance.

For Christians today, it can be easy to avoid things that make us uncomfortable, things that force us to examine ourselves and be honest about what God is pointing out. So many Bibles lay unread, or at the very least, half-read. So many prayer times drift off into distraction. I believe we do this subconsciously at times because to interact with God fully means changing. It is easier not to read the passages that we know we don't really agree with, or the ones that we know are right but we have no intention of obeying.

The book *Giving - Unlocking the Heart of True Stewardship* by John Ortberg, Laurie Pederson, and Judson Poling addresses this so eloquently:

*"The more we allow ourselves to grapple with these unsettling passages, the more we are pierced.*

*Our only options, it seems, are to let Christ wound us until he accomplishes what he wishes, or to avoid his words and his gaze and his presence altogether by staying away from his Word. The latter option is easier in the short run. But no true disciple can really be content with it.*

*By now some readers are long gone and others who remain are uncomfortable. I must admit that I share your discomfort. You may even be thinking, 'I'd rather not deal with these issues. I'm content doing what I'm doing.' But are you really content? Are any of us who know Christ, who have his Spirit within, really content when we haven't fully considered his words? When we haven't completely opened ourselves to what he has for us?*

*Comfortable, perhaps. Complacent, certainly. But not content. I, for one, hate to live with that nagging feeling deep inside that when Jesus called people to follow him he had more in mind than I'm experiencing. I don't want to miss out on what he has for me. If he has really touched your life, I don't think you do either."* [12]

The Old Testament tells the story of God and His people. From Creation to Exodus you see mostly individuals and their relationships with God, but after their years of slavery in Egypt, the Hebrews have become a massive nation. While the patriarchs had their own issues with disobedience, we know they remained faithful to God because in Hebrews 11, the Bible praises them for their faith. But for Israel, although God loved and remained faithful to them, the sad reality of their choices are all too evident in scripture.

From the day they left Egypt, the people grumbled and distrusted God. Exodus 14:11-12 *"Is it because there were no graves in Egypt that you have taken us away to die in the wilderness? Why have you dealt with us in this way, bringing us out of Egypt?"* They complained about water, then they complained about food, then they complained about variety in their food. Each time, God provided them with what they needed in a huge, visual, miraculous way. But they didn't learn to trust Him to meet their needs. They didn't even learn to ask for what they wanted politely. They defaulted straight to complaining and accusing God of abandoning them.

In Exodus 32 they convince Aaron to make an idol for them, literally saying, *"These are your gods, Israel, who brought you up out of Egypt"* and attributing the great works of God to a statue of a cow Aaron had made from their jewelry.

Their lack of faith reaches a climax when they get to Canaan and completely freak out at the current inhabitants of the land. In Numbers 14:11 God says to Moses, *"How long will this people spurn me? And how long will they not believe in me, despite all the signs which I have performed in their midst?"* He decides that, because of their disbelief, no one from this generation except Joshua and Caleb will enter the Promised Land.

Israel is sent back out to the wilderness to wander for 40 years and the rebellion starts again, only it escalates. Korah leads a revolt against Moses and Aaron, ending with the ground opening up and swallowing them and all their families. *The very next day* they are murmuring again, and God sends a plague that wipes out 14,700 of them.

Mere verses later, God delivers enemies into their hands and gives them victory in battle, but as they travel they become impatient and cry out again, *"Why have you brought us up out of Egypt to die in the wilderness? For there is no food and no water, and we loathe this miserable food."* Numbers 21:5.

Back and forth, over and over, Israel refuses to live by faith in God and He punishes them for their hardness of heart. He doesn't turn against them because He hates them, in fact when they do obey He pours out His blessing. He doesn't leave them to serve their 40 year punishment alone, He continues to lead them, teach them, and provide for them--even to the point that their clothes don't wear out and their feet don't swell for the entire journey. (Deuteronomy 8:4)

Their habitual faithlessness didn't cease when they finally entered the Promised Land. They refused to fully drive out the Canaanites; which led to a close proximity to pagan gods and the opportunity to worship them, which they indulged in regularly.

God allowed their enemies to oppress them, but continually saved them when they cried out to Him. *"But as soon as they were at rest, they again did what was evil in your sight. Then you abandoned them to the hand of their enemies so that they ruled over them. And when they cried out to you again, you heard from heaven, and in your compassion you delivered them time after time."* Nehemiah 9:28

They envied the nations around them and in 1 Samuel 8, rejected God's leadership when they asked Samuel to give them a king. What followed

were years and years of different rulers; some of
them were faithful to God, but many were not.
Israel split into the northern kingdom and Judah
became the southern kingdom. Idol worship was
prevalent and, at times, even encouraged by the
monarchy.

Finally, they were overthrown, and many of them
were taken into captivity by Assyria and Babylon.
But even in exile, God doesn't abandon His people.
His mercy and love for this rebellious group is
astounding. So convicting for me.

Looking back at their long history of rebellion
against God, I can identify with the struggle, the
unwillingness to break under His pressure. But
when God finally allows them to be torn from their
home and scattered into exile something changes
for Israel.

For one, they don't return to idol worship. Scholars
have differing opinions as to why that is, but the
redundant issue of worshipping other gods is
absent from scripture after the exile. This could be
because, with the decimation of the temple and
scattering of the tribes, worship became personal
again. People were worshipping in their homes,

gathering in the synagogues, and the prophets during that time (Isaiah, Jeremiah, Ezekiel, etc) were emphasizing the importance of a personal response to God instead of a corporate rote.

Another change is that they started to revere the scriptures again. In 2 Kings 22 we read about King Josiah's high priest finding the book of the law in the temple and when the scribe reads it to him, Josiah tears his clothes. They didn't know their own history and the warnings God had been giving for generations. When Ezra brings out the book of the Law of Moses in Nehemiah 8 and all the assembly listens to him read from daybreak till noon, this is a significant moment for Israel. *"They read from the Book of the Law of God, making it clear and giving the meaning so that the people understood what was being read."* Nehemiah 8:7

God pursues us. And at times it might feel like the pursuit of a predator stalking his next meal. But in reality, he is chasing us down as we run toward a lifetime and possible eternity of separation from Him.

When you finally give up, when your spirit is broken and exhausted and ready to give Him what He asked for in the first place, He offers a gift of mercy. Right when you least deserve it.

Why didn't we just take it to begin with?

We rebel violently against the simple truth that trust and obedience are the only way to be happy in Jesus. They are all He asks for, all He has ever asked us for.

Like God's chosen people, we finally come to the end of ourselves, and there God meets us in an intimate and personal way. As in a marriage, the daily routine of doing life together is where true intimacy is found. I think of the practice of courtship where young men and women are encouraged to get to know each other in groups and avoid time alone to protect themselves from sexual temptation. That's because those personal times alone with the loved one are when walls come down and real communication draws hearts together.

You insulate yourself from that intimacy with God by coming to Him in church but avoiding Him in the privacy of personal prayer and study. Imagine a marriage where the only connection point is in a group setting. Not very personal, is it? You are able to experience and learn and grow in fellowship, but you build your relationship with God in the daily communion.

A monogamous covenant relationship with God is the goal for all believers. Fight the temptation to practice polygamy of religion by holding power or comfort or pleasure in too high esteem.

Has God brought you through a period of exile?

Has he offered you mercy in your lowest hour?

My time of exile was during my 2 years at discipleship school where I finally presented myself to God with full intent to obey. When I submitted to the difficult tasks of brokenness, dependence on His grace, confession, and accountability, that is where God in His mercy changed my heart and turned me away from sin.

# Reflect & Check

*Take a few minutes to pray about and answer these questions. Is God asking you to change, repent, or act differently as a leader or as a Christian?*

———

*What are specific times that God has disciplined you?*

*How has God shown you His love and mercy in the midst of discipline?*

*Ask God if He fully knows you and fully loves you and write down what He says.*

# Chapter Eight

# Come With a Broken Heart

*"You do not delight in sacrifice, or I would bring it…*
*the sacrifices of God are a broken spirit;*
*a broken and contrite heart."*
*- Psalm 51:16-17*

We are getting into the nitty gritty of how to deal with sin. I've had a refresher course in these concepts over the past few weeks because all the old temptations and lies clamoured back into my mind as soon as I started writing this book.

And to tell you the truth, I have not combatted all of them successfully. I have whispers in my ears that no one will respect me, that leaders will look down on me, that my sin nature disqualifies me from ministry. And the old familiar chant that I am a waste of time, money, and resources.

But I can chuckle a little at that now. Because it sounds like Satan is getting desperate.

There are two incredible and life-giving facts about being broken. One is that this is what God wants from you, which we'll talk about later. But the second fact is that when you are broken before God, sin loses its power completely.

Satan has nothing to hold over my head and taunt me with. He doesn't have a bomb to drop. The bombs are all down, the cards are out. The world knows that my brain is wired to escape reality with sensuality. What happens to me if that fact is re-exposed? Nothing really. Maybe an extra opportunity to rejoice in God's grace and marvelous work in my heart. Thank God He saved a wretched sinner like me. Thank God I am not ruled by those passions anymore! By the grace and power of God, I am a new creation. What can the devil do to me?

When Paul says in 1 Corinthians 15:56 *"The sting of death is sin, and the power of sin is the law."* he is telling us this same truth. Christ's work on the cross for us fulfilled the law, and the new requirement for righteousness is to confess and believe in Jesus Christ. Without the law's demands, sin becomes powerless. It still exists, but we are now dead to it's mastery. Without sin's power and penalty, death loses its eternal sting for the believer.

Verse 57 says *"But thanks be to God! He gives us the victory through our Lord Jesus Christ."* Our response when we sin now is to confess, repent, and glory in the forgiveness and victory He has provided for us. We boast in our weakness and let Christ's power be made perfect in them. When I am weak He is strong.

Brokenness says with Paul, *"Christ Jesus came into the world to save sinners--of whom I am the worst."* 1 Timothy 1:15. Notice he doesn't say "of whom I *was* the worst." He says "I *am currently* the worst of sinners." In Romans 7 he goes back and forth with *"For I do not do the good I want to do, but the evil I do not want to do—this I keep on doing."*

There's a freedom in brokenness. Not a license to continue in sin, but a freedom to fall and get back up again with new resolve.

C.S. Lewis gives one of my favorite examples of this: *"[God] wants them to learn to walk and must therefore take away His hand; and if only the will to walk is really there He is pleased even with their stumbles."* [13] You see, it isn't our perfection that God wants, it's our heart, full of a pure desire to please Him. Like a parent watching their child stumble and fall time and time again, He delights in you because you are learning, getting better, and becoming more and more like Jesus.

There is a prayer that I have been lifting to God for a decade now. *Never stop teaching me, Lord.* And His answer is always the same:

*As long as you are willing to be taught.*

Jerry Bridges, in his book *The Pursuit of Holiness* makes this claim, *"...our attitude toward sin is more self-centered than God-centered. We are more concerned about our own "victory" over sin than we are about the fact that our sins grieve the heart of God. We cannot tolerate failure in our struggle with sin chiefly because we are success-oriented, not because we know it is offensive to God"* [14]

In Christian culture we make sin about our own self-control. Fighting temptation seems to be about

*"I can do all things…"* but brokenness of heart is when you come to God saying, *I CAN'T do this.*

One of the ways I tried to cure my sexual temptation was to educate myself about the porn industry and its link to human sex trafficking. Millions of men, women, and children are being forced to perform sexual acts against their will for someone else's pleasure and profit. It's disgusting. And humanity's regular consumption of pornography not only fuels the demand for trafficking, it deepens the degradation of each individual caught up in it. Remember, addictions escalate. So sex workers (both willing and unwilling) are forced to fulfill fantasies that go far beyond a normal sexual encounter. When the beast of addiction needs a new low, Satan finds one.

But my effort to gross myself out with these facts about the sexual exploitation industry wasn't enough to keep me from pornography for long. It just caused an even deeper shame when I would indulge in lust, because I wasn't just hurting myself. I could feel the weight of my participation in the dehumanization of these children of God.

Brokenness isn't an act of willpower, it is an act of faith.

You can't logic away your sin nature or rely on your own morality to keep you from sin. Our hearts are depraved, and we will only ever gravitate toward the darkness on our own strength. True brokenness is the work of and the gift of the Holy Spirit.

In Genesis 4, after Adam and Eve are cast from Eden, they give birth to their first two sons, Cain and Abel. When they were young men they each brought an offering to God. Cain was a farmer, and we are told *"In the course of time Cain brought some of the fruits of the soil..."* His brother Abel brought *"fat portions from some of the firstborn of his flock."* God accepted Abel's offering but rejected the offering that Cain brought before him.

There isn't a clearly stated reason in scripture as to why Cain's offering was rejected. I have read some theories suggesting God had already established the practice of a blood sacrifice and Cain deliberately brought something else, and I have also heard people argue that Cain's produce offering was the leftovers of his harvest and not the first fruits, whereas Abel brought the firstborn from his flock. Hebrews 11:4 gives us a little insight. *"By faith Abel brought God a better offering than Cain did. By faith he was commended as righteous, when God spoke well of his offerings. And by faith Abel still speaks, even though he is dead."* So maybe the difference was all in their approach.

Whatever the reason, Cain reacted to the event with anger. He made his attempt to please God and it was rejected. Then the Lord spoke to him and said, *"Why are you angry? Why is your face downcast? If you do what is right, will you not be accepted? But if you do not do what is right, sin is crouching at your door; it desires to have you, but you must rule over it."*

Cain was given the chance to try again. God didn't reject his offering and then cast him out, He said *"if you do what is right will you not be accepted?"* giving him the chance to regroup and come back to God with a contrite heart. God also warned Cain that sin was crouching in wait, much like 1 Peter 4:8 says of Satan: *"Your enemy the devil prowls around like a roaring lion looking for someone to devour."*

Crouching in wait, prowling, and looking for someone to devour. Cain let his anger fester--Satan took that opportunity--and Cain lashed out, becoming the first murderer in human history.

All because he didn't bring God what He asked for.

You don't get to decide what you want to offer God. He has made clear what He wants from you. The tangible offering might change, but what He requires of us inwardly does not.

Psalm 51:16-17 shows us what God is after: *"For you will not delight in sacrifice, or I would give it; you will not be pleased with a burnt offering. The sacrifices of God are a broken spirit; a broken and contrite heart, O God, you will not despise."*

If all God wanted was an animal without blemish to be slaughtered and used as a burnt offering, the Pharisees would have been doing fine. But even though the details of the sacrifices in Biblical times were very important, it's the heart that God has been after from the beginning.

Hebrews 10 talks about how Israel meticulously followed God's laws about sacrifices, but the law is only a shadow and a reminder of sin. *"Day after day every priest stands and performs his religious duties; again and again he offers the same sacrifices, which can never take away sins."* Hebrews 10:11.

In the same way, when we try to approach God with our works or goodness, it is nothing but a stark reminder of how much we fall short. Israel needed to hear that *"It is impossible for the blood of bulls and goats to take away sins."* Hebrews 10:4. And we need to hear that it is impossible for good intentions, social justice, ministry work, or moral purity to take away sins.

Only the blood of the Lamb of God, poured out for our iniquities is the perfect sacrifice for sin.

What do we have to offer to the equation? Need. Emptiness. Brokenness.

*"God uses broken things. It takes broken soil to produce a crop, broken clouds to give rain, broken grain to give bread, broken bread to give strength. It is the broken alabaster box that gives forth*

*perfume. It is Peter, weeping bitterly, who returns to greater power than ever."* [15]

- Vance Havner

That's the message at the core of the *"rend your heart and not your garments"* verse. God wants you to come to Him broken over your sin, because that is the foundation on which He can build.

I am a planner. When a circumstance in my life changes, my brain is immediately rearranging and recreating the plan. It's a lot like I'm trying to build my dream life for myself like a tower of blocks, stacking each one into place as I plan what my life will look like.

*I can get this job.*

*I can marry this guy.*

*I can be important and respected in this space.*

But God seems to follow me around knocking over my towers and grand plans. The job would fall through, the guy I liked never returned my affection, the people I wanted respect from never noticed me.

It was almost like He was saying, *"I want to **give** you something. And I can't give it to you if your hands are full because you keep taking things for yourself."*

As a mother I can see this so clearly. My daughter has a very short-sighted view of her life, and there are times when she grabs at what she wants even though she has been told no. When I'm looking at her little face, so desperate to possess this thing, I can understand how God feels when He tells me to let go because He has a different plan in mind.

*I want to **give** you something.*

Brokenness has a correct understanding of itself and its role in God's plan. We are His workmanship, we are created for purpose, and God is capable of doing mighty things in our lives. But they aren't going to be things we build out of our own strength. He isn't going to accept sacrifices that we bring without faith, without humility, without a broken and contrite heart.

When you come to God with your idea of sacrifice and your idea of success, 9 times out of 10 you are off base. He wants your heart, broken and ready to be restored and used in *His* plan.

# Reflect & Check

*Take a few minutes to pray about and answer these questions. Is God asking you to change, repent, or act differently as a leader or as a Christian?*

———

*When you are faced with your own ugliness and sin, how do you respond?*

*What are ways that you have tried to please God on your own terms?*

*Ask God what sacrifice He wants from you, and write down what He says.*

*Chapter Nine*

# Grace That is Greater

*"In the same way, count yourselves dead to sin but alive to God in Christ Jesus."*
*- Romans 6:11*

When we present ourselves to God as living sacrifices, completely willing and ready to obey Him, all of heaven must breathe a sigh of relief as God rolls up His sleeves.

*Finally, the work can begin.*

We spend a lot of time either ignoring God or fighting Him. Even after coming to the point where we want to deal with sin, old habits die hard. Much of the actual work of putting sin to death is about relearning habits. But the hardest lesson for me has been finding the balance between my responsibility to change and the mystery of God's grace that does the work of transforming my mind.

It is very easy for Christians to start placing value on the outward signs of holiness instead of the inward work of holiness. We want to be holy, and so we *act* holy. We manufacture the appearance of spiritual maturity because to actually become spiritually mature is a long and humbling process. One friend told me that she felt like she was putting up a front of spiritual maturity and all the while desperately struggling to catch up to the fake version she was presenting to the world.

Grace is the tool that God uses to work the powerful and messy process of transformation in each of his children. His grace should stun us. It should humble us. It should make the facade we put on for the sake of impressing the world fall flat.

God reaches down to us at our lowest, sees us at our ugliest, and surrounds us with a grace that is greater than our very worst sins.

There's an awful lot of talk in the Bible about being dead. You are to put to death the deeds of the flesh, die to yourself, count yourselves dead to sin, you have been crucified with Christ, you are to offer your body as a living sacrifice. All of these verses point to killing our old nature and being brought back to life, just as Christ was raised from the dead to a new nature and purpose.

We cling to life though; to our current lives in their current form that we understand and are comfortable with. We fear death because we don't understand it and don't know what happens next.

My favorite picture of death to self and life in Christ is that of a seed. In John 12:24 Jesus says, *"unless a kernel of wheat falls to the ground and dies, it remains only a single seed. But if it dies, it produces many seeds."* There is a dying that has to happen for growth to occur. The current life in its current form has to pass away in order for God to conform us to the likeness of His Son. There is no other way for us to be like Him.

The mystery of God's transformative grace happens in that death, and so we need to learn to welcome it. As Elisabeth Elliot says, *"We are not meant to die merely in order to be dead. God could not want that for the creatures to whom He has given the breath of life. We die in order to live."* [16]

This is the hardest aspect of dealing with sin, because you can't do the work. The work of new life and a new mind belongs to the Holy Spirit. In so many ways our only job is to stand still and let Him work.

You'll see that this is the Spirit's work in Titus 3:5, *"He saved us through the washing of rebirth and renewal by the Holy Spirit"*, and Romans 12:2, *"be transformed by the renewing of your mind."* And in Ephesians 4:23, *"be renewed in the spirit of your mind."*

That "washing of rebirth and renewal" is also what Ephesians 5 tells us that Christ does for His bride, *"...just as Christ loved the church and gave himself up for her to make her holy, cleansing her by the washing with water through the word.."* When Jesus prays for His disciples in John 17:17, He says, *"Sanctify them by the truth; your word is truth."*

You are sanctified, washed, renewed, and cleansed by the word and the truth of God, which is the work of the Holy Spirit.

What an incredible gift. Not only that He loves us, shows us mercy and saves us, but that He pours out His grace and puts in the work to transforms us into His own new creation. What an undeserved and incredible gift.

Our job then, is to put ourselves in position: on the altar as a living sacrifice. We choose to sacrifice our desires and instead follow Christ into a life of humility and suffering, because that's what it takes to be conformed into His likeness. Our minds are washed and renewed as we follow in His steps.

The death we die to our sin and flesh is one we should be grateful for. Yes, we face death, and it's an honor to face it for His glory. If this is what it takes for God to refine us, let's face it with joy and obedience.

God's powerful grace is what makes the difference in this fight against sin, whether you are talking murder, gossip, adultery, or envy. Our focus has to shift away from the sin and onto God. I have heard many people say this, that we need to stop obsessing over sin and focus our study on God, but we fail when we shift so far off of sin that we don't even really understand it except for arbitrary rules and vague commands. We need to be as wise as serpents (Matthew 10:16) and part of that wisdom is an understanding of what we face.

At the same time, your focus is what determines where you are going. Paul says in Philippians 3:13, *"Forgetting what is behind and straining toward what is ahead, I press on toward the goal to win the prize for which God has called me heavenward in Christ Jesus."*

I don't think what the church needs is more knowledge of what constitutes sin. We've done a lot of nitpicking about what is and is not wrong. Let's table that discussion for a minute. What the church needs is an understanding of how sin works and the strategies to combat it. That's an important foundational and practical knowledge that Christians should have.

But when you are tangled in sin and working to break free, you can't focus and obsess on the sin itself. Amy Carmichael says, *"Do not fight the thing in detail: turn from it. Look ONLY at your Lord. Sing. Read. Work."* [17] There is a distinct difference between understanding our enemy and focusing on our enemy. You must *understand* sin but *focus* on Christ.

Our job is to put ourselves in position for the Spirit to work, and we do that with spiritual disciplines. Exposure to and study of the word of God, time spent before God in prayer, meaningful fellowship with other believers, a practice of confession, tithing, silence, fasting. These disciplines won't save us, but they help us position ourselves on the altar so God can work.

The discipline that has been the most transformative for me is memorizing the word of God. Allowing the Spirit to cleanse me by washing me with the water of the word is instrumental in the transformation of my mind. I can tell when I have lapsed in my memorization. Passages like Romans 6-8, Psalm 119, 2 Peter 1, and Ephesians 2 are ones that I hold close to my heart.

We measure the work of the Spirit in our lives by the fruit that grows as a result of his presence. We should see love, joy, peace, patience, kindness, goodness, faithfulness, and self-control in our lives, not just present, but *growing*. A living God doesn't plant things in His children then leave them stagnant. The gifts of God and the work of God will move and change and grow in us visibly, which is what we call fruit.

All of these things work in accord with each other.

1. The understanding of our sin drives us to the cross
2. We rely on God's grace by practicing disciplines
3. So that He transforms us into the likeness of His Son
4. Which we can measure by the fruit of the Spirit

The temptation is to imitate this sequence with our own works and willpower, forcibly creating an appearance of fruit in an effort to skip the whole sacrifice/death part. But don't do it. Don't miss the wonder of seeing God's true work of transformative grace in your heart for fear of the process.

# Reflect & Check

*Take a few minutes to pray about and answer these questions. Is God asking you to change, repent, or act differently as a leader or as a Christian?*

———

*What are ways that you have manufactured the appearance of spiritual maturity?*

*What example can you point back to and say "THAT was the Holy Spirit's work in my life"?*

*Ask God what scripture passage you need to memorize and write down what He says.*

# Chapter Ten

# How and Why to Confess

*"If I had cherished sin in my heart,
the Lord would not have listened."
- Psalm 66:18*

I've already said that sin thrives in isolation. It's like
a bacteria left alone to grow in a dark moist
container; the longer you leave it there in the back
of your refrigerator, the grosser it will be when you
finally take the lid off. This is why Satan works so
hard to convince you that you are alone in whatever
struggle you face: because isolation creates the
perfect environment for sin to fester.

When you give sin privacy it becomes more
powerful.

Doubt, fear, and guilt also grow when left alone.
You might notice that when you actually start
talking to someone about your fears you have
sudden clarity and they aren't actually as scary as
you've built them up to be in your head.

Confession is like that. When you leave your sin undisturbed in the darkness it seems impossible to ever confess. You live in fear, knowing no one will understand, and everyone you have ever loved will look at you differently. But bring it to light and it loses its power.

There are multiple reasons to bring sin to light:

- So it can become part of your testimony
- For others to know they aren't alone
- Because sin no longer has mastery over you
- Confessed sin is forgiven sin
- To clear your conscience
- So God can be glorified in your weakness
- Because he can work it together for good
- Because the church needs an example
- To demonstrate the power of God

There's only one reason not to bring your sin to light--to protect yourself against God's transformative grace in your life. If you don't want to become a new creation, keep that sin hidden away as long as possible.

I understand the fear of confession. I have been there, and I am there each time I need to confess again. But that fear doesn't hold me back anymore because the freedom on the other side of confession is the most beautiful thing I have ever experienced.

If you are standing in the shadows and living in fear of your sin being exposed, this is God's plea to you:

*Don't wait to get caught.*

*Give yourself up.*

*Turn yourself in.*

Confession feels like a huge wall. You stand on this side with your secret shame, and the only thing keeping you from the help you need is this Thing. This act of speaking aloud your real issues and letting someone else know how ugly your heart actually is. Satan makes that wall feel impossible to breach.

But the thing is, our sin will be exposed. Eventually. Somehow. And if you wait till you get caught it might be at the expense of broken relationships, missed opportunities, or worse.

Confession is coming out of hiding with your hands in the air. Giving yourself up to the mercy of God in an act of obedience.

The insurmountable wall of confession is a mirage constructed by Satan to keep you from utilizing one of the most powerful tools to defeat sin. Confession is not actually a wall at all. It's the open door between a life of secret shame and a life of joyful dependence on God.

The problem isn't that the church doesn't talk about confession, but that when it's mentioned we only talk about it vaguely. We tell people that they need to confess, but we don't give them an avenue to do so. We don't give them the tools to do so. Essentially we let them know there is this vital aspect of faith which good Christians can and should practice on their own. We leave our congregations in a position where their choices are to go find the answers by themselves or ignore the discipline of confession all together.

Think of your church's teaching and strategy about confession. How do you recommend people confess sin? Do you regularly invite people to confess? Do you practice corporate confession as an example for personal confession?

We can intentionally incorporate confession into regular church life. Here are some ideas:

- Do a sermon series on how and why to confess
- Offer altar calls specifically for believers to confess, encouraging spiritually mature believers to exercise this privilege first.
- Form a mentorship/accountability program to encourage longer term confession and accountability
- Have counseling or therapy resources for people struggling with addictive sin
- Participate in confession regularly yourself, and, when appropriate, confess your sin to the congregation
- Train small group leaders to teach and encourage confession of sin in their groups
- Set the expectation that sin is not something to hide
- Offer an anonymous prayer service as a first step for people who are afraid to come forward

- Offer discipleship training classes
- Ask mature believers who have dealt with sin to share their testimonies as a public example of exposing sin & the power of God's grace

You need to get comfortable with the confession of sin. If you are experiencing health problems you don't hide those symptoms from your doctor. You bring the evidence forward so they can give you the best treatment. In the same way, bringing the symptoms of your sin nature into the open allows God to heal you.

There are a lot of questions and concerns about confession that I'll try to address, but in many cases will have to be answered by your individual churches, ministries, and families after a thorough study and time spent in prayer.

**Does all sin need to be confessed?**

This ultimately is between you and God, but here are some questions to consider. Is the sin in your past or are you currently involved in it? Are you plagued with guilt over the sin or does it feel resolved in your spirit with God? Is the Holy Spirit convicting you to confess it?

Confession is not about spilling every wrong thing you've ever done in public. Confession is about breaking the power that sin has in our lives and opening the doors to God's forgiveness and cleansing. *"If we confess our sins, he is faithful and just and will forgive us our sins and purify us from all unrighteousness."* 1 John 1:9

There is no arbitrary line for what needs to be confessed and what doesn't, so if there is sin in your life, pray and ask the Spirit if you need to confess it. If you are willing to obey He will prompt you faithfully and you'll know what is right in your situation.

**Is there a wrong way to confess?**

Yes. Choosing the wrong person to confess to can end up very badly. Confess to a gossip and your private information might end up going further than you intended. Confess to a predator and you might be vulnerable with someone who can use that information to hurt you. Confess to an enabler and you might find commiseration and someone to justify your wrongdoing.

Additionally, confession can be done with a wrong motive. Emotional vulnerability can easily become manipulation. You need to guard against the mentality that confession is sharing a secret. Letting someone in on your "secret" is a dangerous lie. True confession is about bringing something to light, not dragging someone else into the dark.

Confession generally should be between those of the same sex, as vulnerability can quickly lead to attraction. Be aware of the pitfalls and design your official avenues for confession with care. Guard the hearts and minds of your family, congregation, and those you serve by providing safe methods for them to deal with sin.

### What if someone confesses a crime/addiction/etc?

Take the time to learn your area's laws for reporting crimes like child pornography and different types of abuse. Make sure that the people you are directing your church to confess to are trained to know when to contact authorities or recommend professionals for therapy, counseling, or legal help.

Our world is dark. Be prepared for confession to unearth some ugly ugly things.

Confession is a tool to help us throw off the sin that so easily hinders and entangles us. Dropping the burdens of unconfessed sin frees us up to be used by God.

*"Therefore, if anyone cleanses himself from what is dishonorable, he will be a vessel for honorable use, set apart as holy, useful to the master of the house, ready for every good work."* 2 Timothy 2:21. We can cleanse ourselves of what is dishonorable by confessing sin so we are unhindered for God's use.

One of my primary goals in life is to be useful to God. I've spent too long listening to Satan tell me that my sin renders me a useless waste. It means so much every time God prompts me to do something and I am free to obey. If you want to be useful and effective for God's purposes, confession needs to be a regular practice for you.

When you harbor sin in your heart you align yourself with the enemy. You're working on the side of darkness. It doesn't only harm you, it harms the body of Christ as a whole when Christians live with unconfessed sin.

Paul says in Galatians 5:1 *"It is for freedom that Christ has set us free. Stand firm, then, and do not let yourselves be burdened again by a yoke of slavery."* For a child of God who has already been set free, it's a terrible thing to passively let yourself be bound again by sin just because you are afraid of what will happen if people knew what sin really looks like in you. Don't let your fear of the truth be greater than your faith in the Truth.

*Don't wait to get caught.*

Write out your confession first. Get it out of the darkness enough to define it on paper, and pray for the right opportunity and scenario for you to confess.

*Give yourself up.*

Look around you to see how God might be answering your prayer for provision. Does your church have a mentorship program? Are there leaders or mature Christians you know have dealt with sin and are living in obedience? Is there a Christian counselor or therapist you could see? Prayerfully choose the opportunity that God provides for you and set an appointment to talk.

*Turn yourself in.*

You might need to just hand them your written confession if you can't get the words out. But turn yourself in. Push past the invisible wall, through that open door, and start bringing your sin into the light.

The ugliest parts of us need the light of truth more than any other. The jealousy we feel, the anger, the pride, the bitterness, the lust. It's time to unlock the closets where we have been carefully hoarding sin for years and let the Holy Spirit do His cleansing work in us.

And it is your responsibility to set the example. Go first. Bring confession back into practice in your church, in your family. The church is floundering;

many people are trying to find confession and accountability for themselves without the help of spiritually mature leaders who will make sure there is safety and order. You have a heavy responsibility to guide and protect the bride of Christ in the vulnerable act of confession.

*"Gracious God, our sins are too heavy to carry, too real to hide, and too deep to undo. Forgive what our lips tremble to name, what our hearts can no longer bear, and what has become for us a consuming fire of judgment. Set us free from a past that we cannot change; open to us a future in which we can be changed; and grant us grace to grow more and more in your likeness and image, through Jesus Christ, the light of the world. Amen."* [18]

From the PCUSA Book of Common Worship
Louisville: Westminster John Knox, 1993; p. 88

# Reflect & Check

*Take a few minutes to pray about and answer these questions. Is God asking you to change, repent, or act differently as a leader or as a Christian?*

———

*What is your experience with confession?*

*Is there anything in your life that you are afraid for people to find out?*

*Ask God to show you who you should confess to and when, then write down what He says.*

# Chapter Eleven

# Intrusive Accountability

*"And if your hand causes you to sin, cut it off.*
*It is better for you to enter life crippled than with two*
*hands to go to hell."*
*- Mark 9:43*

What do you think of when you hear the word
accountability? Some of you might have the
experience of doing life with a small group of
people, or meeting with someone you can really
share your heart with and you help each other
navigate life in light of your faith in Christ.

But to others, accountability might bring up
memories of awkward conversations with someone
you don't know well. An authority figure who
doesn't feel truly invested in you, or a friend who
gets antsy and isn't sure what to do with the
information you are giving them.

"So, how are you doing with… stuff?"

I have had both good and bad accountability. And I'd like to point out several things that make for good accountability.

**Good accountability is consistent**

Once a month, every week, over phone calls, in person, or video chat… it doesn't matter. Good accountability means you regularly see someone for the purpose of catching up on what is going on with them internally. It doesn't mean every interaction is a deep dive into their past sin, but it means at every interaction the option is open to discuss victories and failures, excitement and frustration in everyday life.

**Good accountability is specific**

A good accountability group or pairing will know what specifically they are praying for and asking about for each person. Unspoken prayer requests are not bad, but when you are dealing with your sin nature and an enemy there isn't time to be vague.

Specific prayer requests and specific questions help in two ways. First, they cut to the heart of the issue, but secondly, they help you avoid sin because you know that you'll be asked about it.

**Good accountability is honest**

If you were perfectly honest it would be easy to keep yourself accountable to change. But the reality is that we are liars, and prone to sin. Our accountability is only as good as we are honest. This means that in order to have effective accountability, we need incentive to be honest. That incentive can be the fellowship of close relationship with someone who knows your struggles and loves you anyway, and the peace of your heart before God.

This makes finding good accountability a hard but important task. You need to find someone who can be consistent, specific, and honest with you, and who will expect you to be the same with them.

I call it "intrusive" because that is what accountability should be. It should thwart that tendency to slip into the shadows and start justifying sin. It should push you toward goals that you set for yourself. It should be a consistent presence in your life that you can rely on for a hug or a kick in the pants, whichever is needed in the moment.

✚

In Mark 9 Jesus says something that always struck me as strange and extreme till I thought of it in light of accountability for sin. He says, *"And if your hand causes you to sin, cut it off. It is better for you to enter life crippled than with two hands to go to hell, to the unquenchable fire. And if your foot causes you to sin, cut it off. It is better for you to enter life lame than with two feet to be thrown into hell. And if your eye causes you to sin, tear it out. It is better for you to enter the kingdom of God with one eye than with two eyes to be thrown into hell."*

Wait, cut it off? Tear it out? The heck are you talking about, Jesus?

But think about those words again with the perspective of how abhorrent God finds our sin. Think about them in relation to the sacrifice of Jesus' blood shed to set us free from sin, and how you crucify Him all over again when you continue to live in it.

Jesus is saying is that it's better to go through life with a handicap than to go through life enslaved to a practice of sin. It's better to go without every physical or emotional happiness, or to be inconvenienced, or to live in a way that doesn't make sense to the people around you. If your goal is holiness it is worth the price you have to pay.

You need to be willing to go to whatever extreme is required to keep you from sin.

A 16 year old girl just started dating the cute bass player in the youth worship band. But she notices that when they hang out together they are getting a little too comfortable touching and kissing. The Holy Spirit is convicting her that this behavior will lead her into sexual sin. So she decides to get a purity ring to remind herself of her commitment to abstain from sexual behavior before marriage. The problem is…the ring isn't helping. She could just give up, and decide that she tried, but it didn't work. But instead she decides to go to her parents and ask them to help her implement some rules about when and how she can be alone with her boyfriend to keep her from getting into these situations. She asks them to keep her accountable and check in with her regularly. Her boyfriend does the same.

For her, this is enough. She has found the level of accountability that will keep her from sin.

A newly married man has been looking at pornography since he was in middle school, and now in his late 20s, he is committed to stopping this sinful practice. He and his wife might choose to put a monitoring and filtering system on their computer and phones to help keep him accountable. But he is tech-savvy and he knows that he can get around the system if he tries. He knows that he needs a more extreme level of accountability to keep him from sin. So he finds a spiritual mentor to meet with regularly, and they pray together and memorize scripture to use when he is tempted. This works for a few months, but he knows that when he gets needy enough he has a tendency to lie. After a few incidents of watching porn again, he decides that he needs to go to the next extreme.

Maybe he gives up data on his phone. Maybe he keeps his computer in a family living space, or only uses it when his wife is home. Maybe he can't have a personal computer. Whatever the extreme measure is that keeps him from sin, that is what he needs to do. And that decision shouldn't be based on what is most comfortable and convenient for him. That decision should be based on what will give him the support he needs to die to his sinful desires.

Good accountability partners help you make these decisions. They pray with you and for you, and listen as you experiment to see where you need to be. Honesty with yourself, with your accountability, and with the Holy Spirit is how you find the extreme that you require. The goal is not to live in that cage forever, but to give God room and time to transform your heart and mind, conforming you into the image of His Son, and cultivating the habits of holiness into your life that will keep you from sin even when your safety nets are not available.

Some examples:
- If your temptation is a love of money, you may need to go to the extreme of giving more away or taking a demotion to remove yourself from the temptation.
- If you tend to gossip, you may need to commit to going to God in prayer before you speak to anyone about what is on your mind, or you may need to commit to asking for forgiveness every time you speak about someone behind their back.

- If you are tempted to sin sexually with a significant other outside of marriage, maybe you need to limit your interactions to group dates. Or if you cannot control yourself, maybe you can't have a significant other at this time in your life.
- If jealousy is what you are dealing with, you may need to unfollow people you are regularly jealous of from your social media. You might commit to praying for them and visiting their pages when your heart is prepared to rejoice and/or weep with them.

None of these examples are the only way to deal with these things, but the point is, there are options. God has made provision for our holiness, He has given us everything we need for life and godliness (2 Peter 1). But are we willing to go to the extreme required for us to be truly holy, or do we dig our heels in and reason that we *deserve* the same freedoms and luxuries that our peers have?

Will you choose to give in to a life of habitual sin, or are you willing to accept a self-inflicted handicap if that is what it takes to keep you from it?

The Spirit does the changing of our hearts, and our responsibility is to put ourselves in position for Him to work. Accountability is a powerful tool to help us continually come back to the altar again. A good accountability partner will walk beside and point you back when you wander.

The local body of Christ is another powerful tool of accountability for believers who regularly worship together. One of the most basic things we need to be held accountable for is our presence.

As a kid I didn't realize the struggle of showing up at church. It was just something we did every week. But as an adult I am faced every week with a wall of excuses for why it isn't vital that I get up and go to church. Just like anything else, regularly being in fellowship with other believers is something that gets more automatic as we cultivate the habit.

I have a great network of Christian women online, and I love the encouragement and iron sharpening iron that goes on there. But God has called me to these people in my local church in a special way. I belong to them and they belong to me. I need them to properly function as a believer in Christ. And my presence or absence affects them just like theirs affects me.

But it's *hard*. It's hard to go spend time with a big group of people. It's hard to build relationships. It's hard to open yourself up to the people who live close to you when the internet has made "finding your tribe" so easy. You need friends that you have to look in the eyes and communicate with. We need each other.

The church is His bride and the fellowship of other believers is where you find deeper accountability, a place to share struggles, conviction for sin and growth, and opportunities to serve and give. The danger is that when so many people are finding fulfillment in friendships and groups and causes outside of the local body, there are fewer and fewer people to enrich the church. When we are busy with long distance friends, we don't feel the need of local ones as keenly. When we are following speakers and podcasters online so much, we don't feel the loss if we can't make it to a Bible study.

But in many churches the focus of the people has shifted from what they can contribute to what they can consume. The staff of the church is sometimes expected to serve everyone because "that's what they are paid for" instead of the body of Christ having a heart to serve each other.

We belong to each other. These are the people God has placed in your sphere and calls you to do life with. His plan for each of your lives is twining together in a unique way that you miss if you keep yourself at a distance.

We need each other. There's something about having people around you to lean on, to bring your fears and failings asking for support, or to cry and pray. We need each other's presence and we need each other's vulnerability and courage to follow Christ.

We affect each other. I served as a worship leader for a small country church when I was in my early 20s, and one thing I learned was that one sincere heart turned toward God could change the atmosphere of the whole group. My obedience or my criticism, my support or my apathy, it either builds the church up or tears it down.

What opportunities are there in your church to connect? How do you reach out to people and invite them to become a functioning member of the body? In what ways do you encourage people to do life together?

✤

In his book *The Pursuit of Holiness*, Jerry Bridges says this:

*"Christians tend to sin out of habit. It is our habit to look out for ourselves instead of others, to retaliate when injured in some way, and to indulge the appetites of our bodies. It is our habit to live for ourselves and not for God. When we become Christians, we do not drop all this overnight. In fact, we will spend the rest of our lives putting off these habits and putting on habits of holiness."* [19]

The forming and breaking down of habits happens in accountability, as you experience the camaraderie of walking through life together. Accountability partners don't change your heart and transform your mind, but they are a consistent presence in your life that says *"we can do this together"*.

And accountability isn't just for dealing with big strongholds of sin. The daily grind of life together means that your accountability people should know your habits and be able to catch and confront before you start slipping.

I was just sharing with my accountability partner a hugely stressful day, and she said to me, "This type of stress is a trigger for you, isn't it?" Yes, it is. We decided on an activity I should spend my evening doing, and I was able not only to avoid sin, but give God significant time that I would not have spent with him otherwise.

Habits are built of 3 components: the trigger, the behavior, and the reward. In my life I know that stress is the trigger that causes me to seek out the behavior of sexual fantasy, and the reward I get from that is an escape from the realities of life.

The secret to changing habits is to replace negative behavior with a more desirable one that gives a similar reward. For example, if I have a stressful day but I turn to prayer instead of fantasy, the reward is that I get to unburden my heart and mind before the throne of God. Just by replacing the behavior of fantasy with the behavior of prayer I get a similar reward emotionally, but in reality it's a much more productive reward because our God is one who answers the prayers of His children.

As we cultivate these good habits in our lives they become easier and easier to do. We need to exercise the muscle of obedience, and that takes discipline and time. Just like physical fitness, it takes consistent repetition to become spiritually disciplined.

The most dangerous thing you can do is assume that you are doing okay. Paul warns, *"So, if you think you are standing firm, be careful that you don't fall!"* 1 Corinthians 10:12. We all need to live with the awareness that we are capable of sin, even sin that we would consider "the worst". Remember when Simon Peter insisted that he would never deny Christ at the Last Supper? Just a few hours later he was eating those words. We need to be diligent in prayer and awareness of potential downfalls. Accountability is a tool that God gives us to help with this. You need the accountability of other believers, and specifically of trusted friends or mentors who are committed to walking with you through life.

✚

When I confessed my porn addiction, I felt like
Satan had been beaten. Finally, I had succeeded in
obeying God and bringing my sin to light. And in
many ways, that was true. But as the years go by, I
recognize more and more what was going on
spiritually in my heart during that time and why I
developed many of the sinful habits that plague me
even today.

I have said that Satan is an opportunist, but I also
recognize now that Satan is a strategist. He is not
randomly shooting temptations at us, he has a plan
that includes retargeting us if we happen to foil his
main attempt.

Satan doesn't need me to be a porn addict in order
to make me ineffective. In fact, I can see that when
I started dealing with the issue of lust in my heart,
that was when I began to struggle in other areas. I
started to overeat, I became obsessed with finding
romantic love, and I became anxious and fearful
that God cared enough about me to provide for my
needs financially.

So when I started to get a handle on porn, Satan retargeted me with other lusts of the flesh that I was not able to recognize as sin because I was so focused on the "big" problem that pornography had become in my life. Please be careful of this retargeting strategy as you learn to deal with sin (1 Corinthians 10:12). Having a trusted person or group who can be praying for you and with you, and who know you well enough to recognize when things seem off is a huge blessing.

Also, I am learning that keeping written record of what God has done, answers to prayer, and patterns of temptation in my life has been a valuable tool to remind myself that I am in a spiritual battle and these events of my life are not random occurrences.

# Reflect & Check

*Take a few minutes to pray about and answer these questions. Is God asking you to change, repent, or act differently as a leader or as a Christian?*

———

*What has been your experience with accountability?*

*Have you gone to every extreme necessary to keep you from recurring or habitual sin?*

*Ask God to reveal habit patterns in your life and show you behaviors to substitute, then write down what He says.*

*Chapter Twelve*

# We Are Forgiven

*"A man with leprosy came and knelt before him and said, 'Lord, if you are willing, you can make me clean.' Jesus reached out his hand and touched the man. 'I am willing,' he said, 'Be clean!'"*
*- Matthew 8:3*

There is a beautiful tension about Christianity. On one hand we are the worst of sinners, completely incapable of saving ourselves or cleansing ourselves from sin. On the other hand, through Christ we are clothed in righteousness and presented pure and blameless before the throne of God.

You need to understand and fully own both of these truths.

It is easy to live in guilt and defeat over our sin, but that was never the purpose of conviction and repentance. Jesus doled out forgiveness of sin like candy to so many people during His ministry. He gives it *freely*. Unlike sanctification, the forgiveness of your sin is not a process you have to go through. Forgiveness is a fact of history. It's already done.

We've spent time talking about confession, accountability, grace, repentance, brokenness, and discipline. Those are all ongoing things in a believer's life. But forgiveness is not. Jesus said, "It is finished." Boom. Forgiven.

I love the story in Matthew 8 where the leper came to Jesus and said, *"Lord, if you are willing you can make me clean."* There wasn't a hesitation or a disclaimer or a caveat to Jesus' response. He just reaches out his hand and touches him, saying, *"I am willing. Be clean."*

*Of course* I am willing. Be clean.

That has *always been* my desire for you.

*Be clean.*

And yet, we don't live as though we are clean. We do an awful lot of wallowing in the past we are ashamed of and/or the current sin we refuse to throw off. What a brilliant attack strategy on Satan's part: to take the gift that God has freely given and make us completely blind to it.

All you have to do is accept the forgiveness.

When I explain this to my four year old, I tell her that Jesus offers us His righteous clothes to wear. When we wear Jesus' righteous clothes, God looks at us and does not see our sin, He sees Christ's righteousness. Trusting that Jesus' work on the cross was enough to pay the price for our sin is how we reach out to take those righteous clothes and slip them on.

But instead, you feel unworthy of the love and forgiveness God offers because of past mistakes and current struggles. You focus on your own failure instead of Christ's victory, and you become wrapped up in yourself, unable to lift your eyes beyond the stress and events of daily life to see God's bigger picture and what you could be doing in it. You see the righteousness that He is offering, but shame keeps you from putting it on.

A Christian who cannot wrap their mind around being forgiven by God will always *feel* defeated by sin.

When I can accept that my sins are forgiven, they are gone. The slate is clean, and I can come running with joy to my Father who loves and delights in me. But if I am focused on my sin, not allowing it to be removed from me as far as the east is from the west, I am acting like a child hiding in fear from a nonexistent threat.

*"As far as God is concerned your sin has ceased to be. He laid it on Jesus Christ your substitute, and he took it and bore the penalty of it — nay the thing itself; he as your scapegoat, carried your sin right away, and it is lost in the wilderness of forgetfulness."* [20] - Charles Spurgeon

Grab that forgiveness and don't let go.

There is so much more to being in relationship with God beyond learning how to deal with sin. We get stuck right out of the gate because we can't get a handle on sin, forgiveness, and sanctification, but He desires to take us further.

Let's stop living as if our sin defines who we are in Christ. He doesn't look at me and see a porn addict, and He doesn't look at you and see your failures either.

✚

When I am hit with a wave of guilt over my sin, and I hear that familiar voice telling me that I am unwelcome at the throne of grace, I remember how the story of the whoring bride always ends.

*"Yet I will remember the covenant I made with you in the days of your youth, and I will establish an everlasting covenant with you."* Ezekiel 16:30

*"Return, faithless people," declares the Lord, "for I am your husband... Then I will give you shepherds after my own heart, who will lead you with knowledge and understanding."* Jeremiah 3:14-15

*"I will plant her for myself in the land; I will show my love to the one I called 'Not my loved one.' I will say to those called 'Not my people,' 'You are my people'; and they will say, 'You are my God.'"* Hosea 2:23

Yes, He disciplines us. But always for the purpose of restoration. The forgiveness of our sin is a fact of history, finished in the work of Christ on the cross. God will always *always* call His children back into fellowship.

Because of Jesus' blood you can come before God covered in the righteousness of Christ and belong there.

I used to cringe when I would read verses like these:

*"...he has reconciled you by Christ's physical body through death to present you holy in his sight, without blemish and free from accusation..."* Colossians 1:22

*"Christ loved the church and gave himself up for her to make her holy... to present her to himself as a radiant church, without stain or wrinkle or any other blemish, but holy and blameless."* Ephesians 5:25b-27

I felt the furthest thing from holy, and my accuser had taught me to accuse myself, so the internal conflict was constant. Without stain or wrinkle, a perfect bride without blemish. Without shame. I couldn't even comprehend that God would see me that way.

But I missed something. I was focused on the finished product: a bride presented to God as blameless. But I didn't see that she was made blameless not by her own effort, but completely through the work of Christ.

*"...he has reconciled you by Christ's physical body through death to present you..."*

*"Christ loved the church and gave himself up for her to make her holy..."*

There is nothing that you can do to make your sin better. It's awful. God abhors it. You and I are both horribly filthy, unfit to walk down the aisle as the bride of Christ. And we can do nothing about it.

He had to do something about it, and He did. It's done. Forgiven. Fact.

Hebrews 10:11-14 shows this, *"Day after day every priest stands and performs his religious duties; again and again he offers the same sacrifices, which can never take away sins. But when this* priest [Jesus] *had offered for all time one sacrifice for sins, he sat down at the right hand of God, and since that time he waits for his enemies to be made his footstool. For by one sacrifice he has made perfect forever those who are being made holy."*

As well as Romans 5:18-19 *"...just as one trespass resulted in condemnation for all people, so also one righteous act resulted in justification and life for all people. For just as through the disobedience of the one man the many were made sinners, so also through the obedience of the one man the many will be made righteous."*

And Colossians 2:13-14 (ESV), *"God made alive together with him, having forgiven us all our trespasses, by canceling the record of debt that stood against us with its legal demands. This he set aside, nailing it to the cross."*

We as leaders need to hold up our lives as an example of what it looks like to stand confidently in the forgiveness of Christ. Not downplaying our sin. Not achieving our own holiness. Not receiving blessing because of our works. Standing with humility and confidence on the work of Jesus Christ at Calvary that instantly cloaks us with His righteousness.

We need to show them. Because if you continue to live with a raincloud of guilt over you, you'll fall back into the same holding pattern that Satan has so many believers trapped in. Never able to move beyond the struggle of daily living and on to God's purposes and plans for us.

Romans 8 starts with a statement of hope for every believer: *"There is therefore now no condemnation for those who are in Christ Jesus."* No condemnation at all. And the reason we don't stand condemned is that the law of the Spirit of life has set us free in Christ from the law of sin and death.

It's not a magical forgiveness of sin. Forgiveness is possible because of the tremendous work--both physical and spiritual work--that Jesus did for us on the cross. The debt that you owe has been paid by someone else.

That's why Paul says in Romans 6:2, "We died to sin, how can we live in it any longer?" There was an astounding price paid to give us a new place to live. Let's move out of sin and into forgiveness.

I get it. It's hard to live in newness of life. And it's really hard to own the righteousness of Christ when you feel like you don't deserve it.

But that is the whole point.

Embrace the fact that you don't deserve it. You need to come to that throne with humility and gratitude that Jesus died for you while you were yet a sinner. At your worst.

Let the depth of your fall be the backdrop against which the height of God's grace is on display.

*"But he said to me, "My grace is sufficient for you, for my power is made perfect in weakness." Therefore I will boast all the more gladly about my weaknesses, so that Christ's power may rest on me. That is why, for Christ's sake, I delight in weaknesses, in insults, in hardships, in persecutions, in difficulties. For when I am weak, then I am strong."* 2 Corinthians 12:9-10

What better display of God's power can there be than His work in a human life plagued by weakness? What better juxtaposition for the grace of God than in the heart of a sinful child who stands condemned by the old written code?

We are the display of His transformative grace in a human heart. And when we can own with humility the truth that we don't deserve His forgiveness in the slightest, that is when He hands it over free of charge.

Too many Christians are afraid to show their weakness, and therefore never experience the power of God made perfect in it.

Will you be the one to stand boldly in your insufficiency and let that power make you strong? Will you be the example to your church of what His power made perfect in weakness looks like in practice?

*Whom shall I send? And who will go for us?*

Here we are, Lord. Send us.

John 8 recounts the story of the woman caught in adultery. The Pharisees bring her before Jesus hoping to catch Him in a trap and He foils their plans like He always did. As the crowd drops their stones and walks away, Jesus asks the woman, *"Where are they? Has no one condemned you?"*

*"No one, sir."* she said.

*"Then neither do I condemn you. Go now and leave your life of sin."*

Read through the gospels and you'll see that Jesus did not do very much condemning of anyone. He had compassion, He healed, He taught, He performed miracles, He forgave sins. He warned about the future. The group He was harshest on were the ones who thought they needed Him the least.

And that's because our sin, though an important thing to deal with, *is not the most important thing.* Sin's importance stems from the fact that it separates us from God and needs to be atoned for. But when we are dealing with sin biblically, we are freed up to see what God has for us next.

Our focus shifts from the barrier to the prize beyond it. Unhindered fellowship with God. Freedom to obey him. A clear conscience. A kingdom focus. There is so much beyond the daily struggle with sin, but so many of us are stuck at that barrier without the tools we need to get up and walk through.

*Come home.*

There is no condemnation for us because the only one with the right to condemn us had a different goal. *"God did not send his Son into the world to condemn the world, but to save the world through him."* John 3:17

So learn to own those truths with confidence: we are the worst of sinners, yet through Christ *"...we have redemption through his blood, the forgiveness of sins, in accordance with the riches of God's grace."* Ephesians 1:7. He isn't condemning us, He is telling us to stop condemning ourselves.

# Reflect & Check

*Take a few minutes to pray about and answer these questions. Is God asking you to change, repent, or act differently as a leader or as a Christian?*

———

*Do you embrace or struggle with the concept of being completely forgiven?*

*What is a specific example where you saw God's power being made perfect in your weakness?*

*Ask God to show you what He sees when He looks at you and write down what He says.*

*Chapter Thirteen*

# Let God Redeem Your Story

*"As I have watched over them to pluck up and break
down, to overthrow, destroy and bring harm,
so I will watch over them to build and to plant,
declares the Lord."*
*- Jeremiah 31:28*

After I confessed my porn addiction and started
letting God transform my mind, there was a long
time when I would look back on the years I spent in
sin and feel like they were wasted. I can recognize
that now as Satan's voice telling me (like always)
that I am a waste.

My God tells me that I am His workmanship.

Even years and years of working through my
addiction and painstakingly creating new habits to
replace the old ones, I still felt a little panicky about
the prospect of anyone knowing that I used to be
addicted to porn. I had shared with one or two

people when I felt prompted to do so, but it was still an area of my life that most people didn't know about.

Then I felt God pushing me to write.

I had resolved never again to tell Him no, so instead I asked Him why. Why now? Why publicly? Why am I putting the worst of me on display?

*Because I am going to redeem it.*

Ten years of my life enslaved to sin. A solid decade that encompassed so much of my childhood. My loss of innocence way too soon. The emotional turmoil and pain. The people and images that haunted me years later.

*I am going to redeem it.*

He was going to redeem my defining shame. He was going to buy my wasted years back from the pit of hell and put them to use on the side of heaven. In that promise He told me that what I considered my worst was going to be the tool He used for His best. He was going to display his strength in my weakness.

Which is perfect, since all I have to offer him is weakness. Thank God He is in the business of renovation, a master craftsman taking what is old and broken and rejuvenating it for new purpose.

You may feel like your past is unusable. Like there is no way that giving your story to God would result in anything but shame and humiliation, but you are wrong. In 1 Corinthians 1:27-29 Paul says, *"But God chose the foolish things of the world to shame the wise; God chose the weak things of the world to shame the strong. God chose the lowly things of this world and the despised things—and the things that are not—to nullify the things that are, so that no one may boast before him."*

He delights in blowing our minds with the transformation. He chooses us, not in spite of our past, but often because of it. Your story may be exactly what He needs to reach a hurting soul.

In Jeremiah 31 we read about the remnant of Israel coming back to Jerusalem, weeping and singing and praising God as He leads them back to the

Promised Land. In verse 28 we read, *"As I have watched over them to pluck up and break down, to overthrow, destroy and bring harm, so I will watch over them to build and to plant, declares the Lord."*

He drove them into exile, plucking them up and breaking them down as he went. But now in His faithfulness He is bringing them back, and not just forgiving them, but building and planting a new work in them again.

Hosea 6:1 shares a similar thought: *"Come, let us return to the Lord; for he has torn us, that he may heal us; he has struck us down, and he will bind us up."*

As I read this, it always strikes me: God will never tear down except to rebuild.

What He is building in us is far more solid and far more beautiful than any of the silly block towers He had to clear away in order to make room to work.

I remember how important my plans felt to me in the moment, how carefully I stacked those blocks on top of each other, trying to build myself a life. I remember how devastated I felt each time God smashed my plans to bits.

But just as He was watching over me to destroy my idea of the life I would lead, He is building and planting the life He has always meant me to lead.

God will never tear down except to rebuild.

We have such a now-centric view of what we want out of life. Our plans revolve around what will get us security and comfort in the moment and for our lifetime. But God's plans for us are in light of eternity. He sees the generational ripples that come from a life of obedience and the children and grandchildren we will influence when we choose to follow Him wholeheartedly.

When you submit to His process, suffer through the tearing down and uprooting and destruction, your heart is fertile ground for the planting.

This is what dying to yourself is all about. It's because His ways are higher, His thoughts are not our thoughts. You die to what you want because you know that His plan is going to be good. We have the deepest faith that He wounds us so that

He can heal us, and He strikes us down in order to bind us up.

In 1 Peter 2 we are told *"...if you suffer for doing good and you endure it, this is commendable before God. To this you were called, because Christ suffered for you, leaving you an example, that you should follow in his steps."*

What He brings us through might be absolutely terrible, and He may break us down to what feels like nothing. But hold onto that truth.

God will never tear down except to rebuild.

We can say with Paul, *"For our light and momentary troubles are achieving for us an eternal glory that far outweighs them all. So we fix our eyes not on what is seen, but on what is unseen, since what is seen is temporary, but what is unseen is eternal."* 2 Corinthians 4:17-18.

He calls us to suffer, but not alone. He is crafting you into something that you won't understand till He's done. But He will always build you back up.

✛

I have talked to so many people who are terrified of their past mistakes ever coming to light. They plan to take their secrets with them to the grave. And I completely understand the sentiment. But God's redemption of my story has given me a new perspective that you might need to hear.

If you don't give him your story, He can't redeem it.

That doesn't mean He'll ask you to write about it or share it with hundreds or millions of people. But you will find the most freedom when you are willing to give Him your story to do with as He pleases.

Just like the old stereotype of people being afraid to give their lives to God in case He does something crazy like sending them to Africa. The thing is, He might. But if He does send you to Africa, He'll give you a heart for the African people and the grace to face whatever it is you'll find there.

When you give God your story, He might not ask you to share it publicly. But if He does, He will give you a heart for the people it will reach and the right words to say. It isn't on us what He does with our stories. All we can do is hold them out with an open hand. And when He asks if you are willing, let your answer always be yes.

In God's hands a story of shame is transformed into a story of grace.

He has done it time and time again, and He deserves our absolute trust that what he asks us to do will work together for our good. Even when we don't understand. Even when we don't see any way it could happen.

It's in His character to take the lowest and raise them up. To make the last become first. To choose the smallest and least qualified and use their obedience to do His great and mighty work.

Who would have thought He'd use a porn addict? I certainly didn't. But it's His prerogative to assign His servants the roles He chooses within His plan.

Your story can be redeemed too. He can take your very worst and glorify Himself through it. If you give Him your ashes, He can make them beautiful.

When God gives us beauty in exchange for our ashes, it's tempting to sweep the ashes under a rug and only show people the beauty. Almost like we are pretending the beauty God gave us is what we had all along.

Doesn't it cheapen the grace of God to pretend like you were already beautiful?

It's because you started out with ashes that you can appreciate how mind-blowing it is that God gives us beauty. The good news of the gospel is that while we were yet sinners Christ died for us, and that story has to include our ugliness in order for Christ's sacrifice to make sense. When Paul says "I will boast all the more gladly about my weakness for when I am weak He is strong" he shows you that contrast between where God has pulled us from and where He has brought us to.

That contrast is what gives other people hope. It is what they can identify with and realize that the good news is for them too. That transition between ashes and beauty is the power of the gospel displayed in us. And when you are ashamed of the past, you are doing your best to diminish the power of the gospel in your own life. When you try to erase the ashes you handicap yourself as you share the gospel.

✝

Out of all the scriptures, the one closest to my heart is Isaiah 61:3. It reads, *"They will be called oaks of righteousness, the planting of the Lord, that he may be glorified."*

I was told once that you won't always see the full grown oaks of righteousness in a person, or even in yourself. But you can look for the seeds. Look carefully and you will see the seeds of righteousness God has planted and is in the process of nurturing into an oak.

An oak tree is tall and strong, a fixture of the landscape. It weathers intense heat, frigid winters, storms, and drought without moving.

Initially, the growth of a tree is visible. You can see it grow from seedling to sapling and each year its trunk and branches fill out and reach up. After awhile you might not be able to see the growth as dramatically, but you know that year after year rings are added inside that tree to mark the time.

An oak of righteousness, the planting of the Lord. Can you imagine that being said of you? Can you imagine being remembered as someone who was immovable in their faith, steadfast in their obedience and trust of the Savior? This, above all else, is what I long for. When I die, let me be worthy of these words engraved on my tombstone. That my life was like an oak of righteousness, a faithful testament to the glory of God.

God plants the seeds of righteousness in every believer and nurtures them. He tills the ground, provides Himself as the light of the world and the living water. He prunes where it's needed.

Our actions and choices right now impact the growth of righteousness in our lives. We decide if we'll let God grow an oak of righteousness in us for His glory.

Will you?

✚

God is asking you to rend your heart. Not a flashy display of conviction on social media, but a somber mourning and repentance as you recognize sin.

You might be a Pharisee, thinking that you've been doing pretty good and this book was written to other people.

You might be a secret sinner trying desperately to find the courage to come clean about the demons you face every day.

You might be a faithful follower, humbled and broken by your own failings and willing to obey when God convicts your heart.

Whoever you are, this message is yours. It is either a refresher, a confirmation, or a revelation of the truth laid out in the Bible about sin and sanctification. Let God speak to your heart as you contemplate the truth you read here.

He is faithful to teach you as long as you are willing to be taught.

# Reflect & Check

*Take a few minutes to pray about and answer these questions. Is God asking you to change, repent, or act differently as a leader or as a Christian?*

———

*What story of yours seems the least likely to be used by God?*

*What is holding you back from giving God that story?*
*How can you release it to Him for His glory?*

*Ask God to use your life as a display of His glory and write down what He says.*

# Acknowledgments

There are so many people to thank, it's ridiculous.

Starting at the beginning, all glory and praise and honor needs to go to my Lord Jesus Christ. We've been on quite the journey together, and it is my joy to walk in His steps.

To my parents and siblings, thank you for your love and support. Even when you had no idea what was going on with me, you were watering the seeds of righteousness that God had planted. Without your framework of a loving and godly family I don't know where I would be.

Sarah, the best of sisters. Thank you for the years of best friendship, the late nights, the tears, and the constant love.

My youth leaders, especially Pastor Ken Keller and Pastor Ken Williamson, I love you guys so much. Your leadership shaped my adolescence and young adulthood in eternal ways.

To the staff at Miracle Mountain Ranch and the apprentices from '04-'05 and '06-'07, your impact in my life has been profound. In so many ways I was back at square one and learning the basics of Christianity all over again, and I had a safe place to do that thanks to you.

Chip and Sandy Hungerford, thank you for being my advisors and another set of parents to me. For reading years of my journals and helping me sort through the mess in my head and heart. And for consistently pointing me to Jesus. Thank you.

To Jason, thank you for loving me when I am at my worst. You have seen the ugliest parts of me and you have seen the very best, and God has used you so many times as he teaches me more about Himself.

My Eden Jane, you are the best gift I have ever been given and it is my greatest honor to be your mom.

To every friend who talked with me about sin over the years, these thoughts were honed in those conversations. People who come to mind specifically are Liz, Amanda, and Angela.

My sister in law, Steffani. You became essential to me so quickly. Thank you for reading my drafts, and for sharing your life, heart, and thoughts with me.

To my soulies, the Christian Creative Mastermind. All the crying emojis, guys. This book would not have been written without you.

Bethany Johnson, thank you for that tiny conversation about how to write an outline that spurred two months of cranking out the first draft. Who knew that God would use that 5 minutes to propel me into action?

Audra Coats-Hudson, thank you for the hours on the phone every week talking over vision and business and marriage and motherhood. I lean on your wisdom and insight for so much.

Heather Owen. You read every chapter as I finished it and kept me on track and on point. God knew what He was doing when He put you in my life. Thank you for keeping me accountable.

# Notes

*Introduction: There's a Porn Addict in Your Church*

1. Miracle Mountain Ranch is a Christian retreat center in Spring Creek, PA. They have a gap year program called the School of Discipleship. You can find out more at www.schoolofdiscipleship.org

*Chapter 2: Teaching Kids About Sin*

2. "precedent." *Merriam-Webster.com*. 2018. https://www.merriam-webster.com (27 June 2018).

3. Elliot, Elisabeth. Passion & Purity: Learning to Bring Your Love Life Under Christ's Control. Grand Rapids, MI: Revell, 1984, 2002.

*Chapter 3: How God Defines Sin*

4. Klein, Patricia S, Forward. Lewis, C. S. Virtue and Vice. New York, NY: HarperCollins, 2005.

*Chapter 5: Recognizing a Secret Sinner*

5. Spurgeon, Charles. "A Divided Heart." The Spurgeon Center. https://www.spurgeon.org/resource-library/sermons/a-divided-heart (retrieved June 27, 2018)

6. Silvoso, Ed. That None Should Perish. Ventura, CA: Regal Books, 1994.

7. Elliot, Elisabeth. "Leaving Self Behind." Revive Our Hearts Radio. https://www.reviveourhearts.com/radio/revive-our-hearts/leaving-self-behind-elisabeth-elliot/ (retrieved June 27, 2018)

8. Reed, Jim (Lead Pastor, New Life Community Church). (2018, September 9). *Destroyed // Destroying Strongholds* [Podcast]. Retrieved from https://itunes.apple.com/us/podcast/destroyed-destroying-strongholds/id1068609976

*Chapter 6: The Father of Lies*

9. Elliot, Elisabeth. A Chance to Die, Reprinted Edition. Grand Rapids, MI: Revell, 2005.

10. Lewis, C. S. The Screwtape Letters. New York, NY: HarperCollins, 2001.

11. Spurgeon, Charles. "The Sword of the Spirit." The Spurgeon Archive. http://www.romans45.org/spurgeon/sermons/2201.htm (retrieved June 27, 2018)

Chapter 7: The Mercy of Discipline

12. Ortberg, John, Pederson, Laurie, Poling, Judson. Giving - Unlocking the Heart of True Stewardship. Grand Rapids, MI: Zondervan, 2000.

Chapter 8: Come With a Broken Heart

13. Lewis, C. S. The Screwtape Letters. New York, NY: HarperCollins, 2001.

14. Bridges, Jerry. The Pursuit of Holiness. Colorado Springs, CO: NavPress, 1996.

15. Havner, Vance. Hearts Afire. Westwood, NJ: Revell, 1952.

Chapter 9: Grace That is Greater

16. Elliot, Elisabeth. Passion & Purity: Learning to Bring Your Love Life Under Christ's Control. Grand Rapids, MI: Revell, 1984, 2002.

17. Skoglund, Elizabeth R. Amma, The Life & Words of Amy Carmichael. Eugene, OR: Wipf and Stock Publishers, 2014.

*Chapter 10: How and Why to Confess*

18. PCUSA Book of Common Worship. Louisville: Westminster John Knox, 1993; p. 88

*Chapter 11: Intrusive Accountability*

19. Bridges, Jerry. The Pursuit of Holiness. Colorado Springs, CO: NavPress, 1996.

*Chapter 12: We Are Forgiven*

20. Spurgeon, Charles. "The Heart Full and The Mouth Closed." The Charles Spurgeon Sermon Collection. http://thekingdomcollective.com/spurgeon/sermon/1289/ (retrieved June 27, 2018)

# About the Author

Hey, I'm Beth! I live in Pennsylvania with my husband and daughter, where I'm involved in my local church and work from home as a marketer for small businesses and entrepreneurs. My life isn't glamorous, but I'm working to submit and obey the Holy Spirit every day as He makes me more and more like Jesus.

I'd love to chat! If you have questions or would like to book me to speak at your event, contact info@rendyourheartbook.com

You can also find more from me at www.rendyourheartbook.com or on Facebook, Twitter and Instagram.

56423945R00130

Made in the USA
Middletown, DE
21 July 2019